# STUDY GUIDE

## ALASTAIR YOUNGER
*University of Ottawa*

# P S Y C H O L O G Y

## M I N D ,  B R A I N ,  &  C U L T U R E

### SECOND EDITION

## D R E W  W E S T E N
*Harvard University*

### EDITED BY THE PRINCETON REVIEW

## JOHN WILEY & SONS, INC.
New York • Chichester • Weinheim • Brisbane • Singapore • Toronto

## Acknowledgements

I wish to express my thanks to Darlene Worth Gavin for her help in writing a number of excellent exercises and questions that appear in the study guide. I am also grateful to Manal Guirguis for diligently comparing between the first and second editions of the text.

ISBN 0-471-32201-6

Printed in the United States of America

10 9 8 7 6 5 4

Printed and bound by Bradford & Bigelow, Inc.

# Preface

The Princeton Review, the nation's leading test preparation company, helps more than half the students entering college and graduate school each year. It prepares students for admissions tests at the high school, college and professional level through books, software, online resources, and live course instruction. We pride ourselves in providing the highest quality instructional material for our teachers.

We have carefully edited and reviewed this Study Guide to accompany *Psychology: Mind, Brain, and Culture*, Second Edition by Drew Westen. We think it is an excellent learning tool for students and it will enhance their performance in class.

- The Editors of The Princeton Review

# CONTENTS

# HOW TO USE THIS STUDY GUIDE

Congratulations on having purchased the study guide to accompany *Psychology: Mind, Brain, and Culture* (2nd edition) by Drew Westen. The purpose of this guide is to get you actively involved in learning the material in your textbook. Its goal is to help you better understand and apply the concepts from the book. Proper use of the study guide, therefore, will enhance your learning of psychology as it is delineated in this well-written textbook by Westen.

The study guide has been designed to facilitate *active* learning. For many students, learning and studying are all-too-often passive rather than active processes. Attending class, reading the textbook, and so on, are, of course, important parts of learning, but most of these activities place students in the role of passive recipient of knowledge rather than active participant in learning. Even when studying, many students simply reread what they have highlighted, recopy their notes, and so on. These strategies lack active integration of knowledge and diagnostic testing of information.

By contrast, active learning requires that students take control of the learning process. Taking control of the learning process means studying in a manner that facilitates *learning*, not superficial memorization. Specifically, actively learning psychology from your Westen textbook requires previewing your textbook to identify exactly where the book and the course are going, pre-reading each chapter before you read it so you can maximize your reading comprehension, working the chapter as opposed to simply reading it, reviewing what you have learned after you read a chapter, and testing your knowledge on an on-going basis so that it becomes committed to memory.

This study guide provides you with specific guidelines for previewing the textbook, pre-reading and working each chapter, and reviewing what you have learned. It also incorporates a variety of diagnostic exercises that will enable you to evaluate what you have learned and "zero in" on areas in which you need to improve. Finally, it outlines an effective method for exam preparation based on the knowledge you have garnered from working through this guide.

The following outline details exactly how to get the most out of this study guide and the Westen psychology text. Take the time to read through each point and incorporate the suggestions. Most of all, enjoy learning about psychology!

## Preview The Textbook

How often have you skipped over all the introductory stuff in a textbook and instead started reading chapter one so you could "get to it." Believe it or not, there is a reason for all that introductory stuff, and skipping it makes learning the content of the book harder. Before you begin reading chapter one, take a little time to preview the book. Begin by reading the author's preface. It will tell you how the book is laid out, why it's laid out that way, and what to expect in each chapter.

Next, read the detailed table of contents so you can see what the author was talking about. Take out your course syllabus and compare it to the table of contents. How does your professor plan to use the textbook? Will you be covering one chapter per week, one chapter per class, or multiple chapters per class? Do you need to know a chapter inside-and-out before class so you can discuss it, or are you reading the textbook as supplemental material to topics covered in class? When will you be tested? Can you tell from the syllabus how many chapters are covered on an exam? Mark dates and as much information as you can on the table of contents so you know exactly when you need to do what.

Combine this information to create a "time line" of the semester. You may even wish to create a master calendar of all your courses, so you can determine crunch times, etc. Let's face it—in a perfect world, you would study as little as possible to learn as much as you can. Doing a little work up front will enable you to balance all the stuff you have going on, do well in your courses, and still have time for an occasional social activity.

**Chapter By Chapter**
There are three parts to actively learning each chapter. First, **pre-read and work** the chapter. Second, **review and learn** the content. Third, **test and know** the material.

**Pre-read and Work**
Why is it easier to read about a subject with which you are familiar than about a totally foreign topic? The more you know about something, the easier it is for your brain to process related information (after studying chapters 3-6, you'll know exactly why this is true). Therefore, to get the most out of your reading, you need to know—before you read it—what it's going to be about. If you read a chapter without having any idea what's going to be covered or what important information will show up, it will be easy to get lost in the details of the chapter and miss the salient points. Also, it is very difficult upon first read to comprehend complex material that's full of unfamiliar jargon. Therefore, to maximize your reading, pre-read each chapter so you recognize important stuff when you come to it.

How do you pre-read a chapter? First, open to the appropriate chapter in the book and corresponding study guide chapter. Carefully read the table of contents at the front of the chapter in the book. Then flip to the summary at the end of the chapter and carefully read each point. This will give you a good idea of the important points of this chapter . Although you won't remember all these points, you will recognize many of them when you read the chapter. This recognition will enhance your ability to assimilate the important information in the chapter more quickly.

Now you are ready to begin to "work" the first segment of the chapter. (Note: If a segment is long or covers particularly dense material, you may wish to read the author's interim summary before you read the segment). Working a segment means actively reading while keeping an eye on what you are trying to glean from the text. As you read, jot down your questions, comments, and notes in the space provided in the **Outline** section of the study guide, and make note of the important terms you come across. Include page numbers of and references to difficult material that you know you will need to review. After you have finished your reading, turn to the **Learning Objectives**. These objectives take the form of short-answer questions. After reading the chapter, check off the questions you are confident that you can answer well. Review the material in the textbook for the questions about which you are less confident, recording the important points from your reading in the space below each question.

### Review and Learn
After you finish working a chapter, you need to take time to really learn the material. This cannot be done immediately after you read the chapter. If possible, wait a day and then review the content of the chapter you read. If you need to do it all in one night, take a break or do some other homework that is completely different from this text.

To review a chapter, reread your answers to the learning objectives questions and key terms, plus your notes. Flip back to any parts of the text about which you feel less-than-confident and reread them. Also, reread the author's interim summaries and end-of-chapter summaries. Mark any areas that seem difficult or confusing to you so you can review them again in the future.

Once you have reviewed the material, apply your knowledge *without referring back to the textbook*. Define the **Key Terms** and do the **Fill-in Exercises**. Then, do the **Application** and **Using What You Have Learned** exercises.

As you work, mark any of the terms or questions that give you difficulty. Once you have finished an exercise, go back to your notes to find answers to the questions that gave you trouble. If you need to, go back to the textbook to find the answers. Finally, check your terms by flipping through the textbook or reading the end-of-chapter summary and the fill-ins by referring to the answer key.

Why should you find the answers to difficult questions on your own as opposed to checking the answer key? The idea of these exercises is to help you commit this information to memory, to really *learn* the content of the chapter. If you were to simply check your work against an answer key, you would not be actively learning. The more clear you are about *why* an answer is right, the more likely you are to understand and remember it. This goes for questions you answered correctly by virtue of a "lucky guess." If you guessed on a question, mark it as a guess and verify it by looking back to your notes and the textbook.

### Test and Know
On a separate day (preferably after some period of time has lapsed), test yourself using the **Sample Questions**. You may wish to mark your answers on a separate sheet of

paper, and take this test again before you have an exam in class (see "Exam Review Strategy" later in this chapter for more exam prep ideas). Again, when you check your answers, review the information thoroughly. Getting questions right is good; knowing why they are right is better.

Upon completing these three parts to active learning, the information contained in a chapter will be stuff you *know*, not stuff you have temporarily memorized for a test. As you work through subsequent chapters, go back and review parts of earlier chapters as needed. The chapters in your textbook build on each other, so reviewing earlier concepts will be easy. If you continually review the concepts you have learned, you won't need to "cram for the exam," because you will know most of the information cold. You may need to review complicated concepts and terms, but you shouldn't need to reread the basic stuff.

Sounds like an awful lot of work, right? Active learning does require more effort. However, imagine instead taking a passive approach to learning this stuff. You read the book. You highlight stuff. Midterms come and you have nine chapters (over 350 pages) of stuff to reread and relearn in one day to be ready for the exam, not to mention that you also have four other major courses to cram for and tickets to the concert of the year. Active learning requires more investment up front, but pays off big in the end. Given that you have to read the stuff anyway, why not take the time to learn it the first time?

**Exam Review Strategy**
If you have consistently worked with this study guide, exam preparation will involve:
- Testing yourself
- Reviewing your notes on each chapter
- Reviewing tricky terms
- Rereading difficult segments (previously indicated by you)
- Rereading the interim summaries and end-of-chapter summaries
- Testing yourself

First test how well you have learned the information by giving yourself a mini-exam. To create a mini-exam, rework the Key Terms, Learning Objectives, and Sample Questions for each chapter (cover your answers or have a friend ask you the questions).

Once you take the mini-exam, you will know exactly how much studying you need to do. Review and reread what you need to (for the most thorough review, follow the outline above). This review shouldn't take long since you've done all the pre-work. After you finish your review, take your mini-exam again, or have a classmate "quiz you" on stuff from the chapters in the textbook. Then, go ace that exam!

Hopefully you will find this study guide a useful tool which enables you to truly learn psychology as it is presented in your textbook. Good luck in your course. This is a great psychology text—enjoy learning about psychology!

# Chapter 1
# PSYCHOLOGY: THE STUDY OF MENTAL PROCESSES AND BEHAVIOR

**PART ONE:** **PRE-READ AND WORK**
**OUTLINE AND LEARNING OBJECTIVES**

Pre-read this chapter's table of contents and end-of-chapter summary. Then, use the outline segment-by-segment to help you work through the chapter. Jot down your own questions, comments, and notes in the space provided. Make a note of key terms and of difficult areas that you will need to review (include page numbers). Then, answer the questions in the learning objectives section that follows. Check off those you are confident that you can answer well. Re-read the material in the text for the questions about which you are less confident. Record the important points from your reading in the space below each question.

## OUTLINE

I. THE BOUNDARIES AND BORDERS OF PSYCHOLOGY

A. **From Mind to Brain:** The Boundary with Biology

B. **A Global Vista:** The Boundary with Culture

C. From Philosophy to Psychology

II. PERSPECTIVES IN PSYCHOLOGY

A. Paradigms and Psychological Perspectives

B. The Psychodynamic Perspective

C. The Behaviorist Perspective

D. The Cognitive Perspective

E. The Evolutionary Perspective

F. Putting Psychological Perspectives in Perspective

G. **Commentary:** How to Grasp an Elephant Without Getting Skewered on the Tusks

## LEARNING OBJECTIVES

Upon completion of Chapter 1, you should be able to answer the following questions.

1.    What is the issue of localization of function in the brain?

has to do with witch parts of the ~~brain~~ brain controls witch functions.

2.    What are the two types of aphasias described by Paul Broca and Carl Wernicke?

Broca- front left hemisphere - ~~~~ understand language, but not speak fluently
Wernicke- behind Broca's area - not understand language or speak

3.  What are the similarities and differences between psychological anthropology and cross-cultural psychology?

*PA - study psychological phenomena in other cultures by observing people in their natural setting. CCP -test hypotheses (psych) in different cultures.*

4.  How are both free-will and determinism evident in much of a person's behavior and characteristics?

*FW- we freely choose our actions (we are in control)*
*D- behavior is caused by outside things.*

5.  In what ways did functionalism differ from structuralism?

*S - experimentation is the only appropriate method for a sciece of psych. (contents of the mind)*
*F- role of function of a psych. process for adapting*

6.  What are the three key components of a paradigm?

*Model or abstract picture of the object of study.*
*Metaphors - for comparison*
*Methods - produce valid & useful data.*

7.  According to Kuhn, how do the social sciences differ from the natural sciences?




8.  What are the three basic assumptions of psychodynamic psychologists?




9.  Briefly describe the methods and data of the psychodynamic perspective.




10.  In what ways does the behaviorist perspective differ from Decartes's philosophical perspective?




11.  How does the behaviorist view of the subject matter and research methods of psychology differ from that of the psychodynamic and structuralist schools of thought?




12.  Why has behaviorism sometimes been called "black-box" psychology?

13.    How do cognitive psychologists employ the metaphor of the computer to understand and model the way the mind works?

14.    What are the similarities and differences between the behaviorist perspective and the cognitive perspective?

15.    Briefly explain the relation between adaptation and niches.

16.    Why have many psychologists from other perspectives criticized the research methods commonly used by evolutionary psychologists?

17.    What are the major concerns of each of the following subfields of psychology?

Biopsychology

Developmental psychology

Social psychology

Clinical psychology

Cognitive psychology

Industrial/organizational psychology

Experimental psychology

Health psychology

## Part Two: Review and Learn
## Key Terms, Fill-In Exercises, Application and Using What You Have Learned

Before doing the exercises below, review the information you learned in this chapter. Reread the work you did in part one of this study guide chapter, plus the interim summaries and end-of-chapter summary in your textbook. Review any problem areas. Once you feel comfortable with the material, do the following exercises without referring to your notes or textbook. If you have difficulty with a term or question, mark it and come back to it. When you have finished an exercise, go back to your notes and the textbook to find the answers to the questions that gave you difficulty. Finally, check your answers (key terms against the textbook and the rest against the answer key).

## Key Terms

Psychology _____

_____

Biopsychology (or Behavioral neuroscience) _____

_____

Localization of function _____

_____

Psychological anthropologists _____

_____

Cross-cultural psychology _____

_____

Free will versus determinism _____

_____

Mind-body problem _____

_____

Introspection _____

_____

Structuralism _____

_____

Functionalism _____

_____

Gestalt psychology _____

_____

Paradigm _____

_____

Model _____

_____

Psychodynamic perspective _____

_____

Behaviorist perspective _____

_____

Cognitive perspective _____

_____

Evolutionary perspective _____

_____

Psychoanalysis _____

_____

Psychodynamics _____

_____

Repress _____

_____

Behaviorism _____

_____

Cartesian dualism _____

_____

Cognition _____

_____

Information processing _____

_____

Rationalist _____

_____

Nature-nurture controversy _____

_____

Natural selection _____

_____

Adaptive _____

_____

Ethology    _____

_____

Sociobiology _____

_____

Evolutionary psychologists    _____

_____

Behavioral genetics _____

_____

Reproductive success    _____

_____

Inclusive fitness    _____

_____

Empiricism    _____

_____

Cognitive behavioral approach    _____

_____

## FILL-IN EXERCISES

Fill in the word or words that best fit in the spaces below.

1.    The degree to which inborn processes determine human behavior is a classic issue in psychology, called the _____-_____ controversy.

2.    John Locke, the seventeenth century British philosopher, contended that at birth the mind is a _____ _____ upon which experience writes itself.

3.   Freud emphasized that much of people's actions is the result of _____ conflicts and compromises.

4.   The psychodynamic perspective lends itself to the _____-_____ method, which entails in-depth observation of a small number of people.

5.   Behaviorism focuses on the relation between objects or events in the environment, referred to as _____, and an organism's response to those events.

6.   The attempt to understand the way conscious sensations, feelings, and images fit together was emphasized by an early school of thought known as _____.

7.   Wilhelm Wundt, viewed by some as the _____ of psychology, emphasized a research method known as _____, in which trained subjects verbally reported everything that went through their minds when presented with a stimulus or task.

8.   The primary method of behaviorism is the _____ method.

9.   Many behaviorists view the mind as a _____ _____ whose mechanisms can never be observed.

10.  Skinner believed that all behavior can ultimately be understood as _____ responses to _____ events.

11.  Skinner observed that the behaviors of organisms can be controlled by environmental conditions that either _____ or _____ their likelihood of occurring.

12.  Many cognitive psychologists view thinking as a form of _____ _____, using the metaphor of the computer to understand and model the way the mind works.

13.  Cognitive psychologists have shown _____ (more/less) interest in the questions raised by rationalist philosophers than have the behaviorists.

14.  Like behaviorists, cognitive psychologists employ _____ methods as their primary research method.

15.  The basic notion of sociobiological theory, common to all evolutionary theories, is that evolution selects creatures that maximize their _____ success.

16.  The theory of natural selection suggests that natural forces select traits in organisms that are _____.

17.    Organisms with fewer adaptive features for their particular _____, or environmental circumstance, are less likely to survive and reproduce.

18.    Conrad Lorenz hypothesized that jackdaws have an inborn or _____ tendency to become distressed whenever they see a creature dangling a black object resembling a jackdaw.

19.    The belief that the road to scientific knowledge is systematic observation is a(n) _____ view of psychology

20.    The field of study that examines interactions of individual psychology and social phenomena is referred to as _____ _____.

## APPLICATION

Consider the following explanations for anxiety. Which theory would be best associated with each explanation?

1.    At one point in time, anxiety was very adaptive, as it prepared us to either fight or flee from situations where real danger was present. In our current society, often neither fighting nor fleeing is a viable option.

2.    Anxiety comes about because certain environmental stimuli have been associated with negative or harmful consequences. The stimulus, therefore, comes to trigger an automatic fear response.

3.    Anxiety comes about because we develop negative expectations about what will likely happen in a particular situation. These expectations cause us to pay close attention to signs of potential harm and to process such information more easily than other information around us.

4.    Anxiety may come about from wishes or fears that we have put out of conscious awareness. We may not even be aware of why we are anxious.

## USING WHAT YOU HAVE LEARNED

Chapter 1 presents four theoretical perspectives in psychology: psychodynamic, behaviorist, cognitive, and evolutionary. At first each seems to conflict with the others. Yet, as the author points out, often one approach complements another -- asks questions the other approach overlooks or adds information not addressed by the other approach. Spend some time reviewing each approach. Can you see their complementarity?

Try applying each approach to some aspect of your own life. Think, for example, about how you responded in a particular situation recently.

1.  Can you imagine the role of unconscious desires or attitudes, or some long forgotten conflict from your childhood (the psychodynamic perspective) influencing your behavior?

2.  What about prior experience? How does your experience with similar situations and the consequences associated with similar behavior (the behaviorist perspective) influence your current behavior?

3.  Consider how you interpret the circumstances surrounding your behavior, how others react to you, what you pay attention to in their reactions, and so on (the cognitive perspective).

4.  Finally, can you see any possible survival value in your behavior (the evolutionary perspective). If not, could it be that this behavior might have been adaptive in a different niche?

## PART THREE:  TEST AND KNOW
## SAMPLE TEST QUESTIONS

Test how well you have learned this chapter's material by answering the sample test questions. You may wish to mark your answers on a separate sheet of paper so you can reuse this test for exam review. Once you have completed the exam, check your answers and then go back to your notes and the textbook to review questions you found difficult.

1.  To understand an individual at a given point in time, psychologists must track

    a.  biological events
    b.  psychological experience
    c.  the cultural context
    d.  all of the above

2.  Carl Wernicke observed that individuals with damage to an area toward the rear of the left hemisphere

    a.  were often unable to speak fluently but could comprehend language
    b.  were able to speak comprehensibly but could not comprehend language
    c.  could both speak fluently and comprehend well
    d.  were unable to comprehend language or speak comprehensibly

3.    Cross-cultural psychologists believe that

   a.    much of the findings of research on topics such as memory, motivation, psychological disorders,  may be culturally specific, rather than universal.
   b.    the only important findings concerning psychological processes are those that hold true across cultures.
   c.    all psychological processes are culturally specific; nothing is universal.
   d.    all psychological processes involve an equal balance between the individual and his or her culture.

4.    The notion that perception involves imposing order on an overwhelming panorama of details by seeing them as parts of larger wholes, was held by

   a.    structuralists
   b.    psychodynamic psychologists
   c.    Gestalt psychologists
   d.    ethologists

5.    "Do people make free choices, or are their actions determined by forces from outside their control?" This philosophical view is know as

   a.    rationalism versus empiricism
   b.    individualism versus relationality
   c.    free will versus determinism
   d.    nature versus nurture

6.    Whereas Wundt and Tichener were associated with the structuralist school of psychology, William James was a _____.

   a.    sociobiologist
   b.    psychoanalyst
   c.    functionalist
   d.    cognitive-behaviorist

7.    Which of the following is not a key component of a paradigm?

   a.    It includes a set of findings that will be considered acceptable by the scientific community.
   b.    It includes a set of theoretical assumptions that provide a model of the object of study.
   c.    It includes a set of shared metaphors that compare the object under investigation to another that is readily apprehended.
   d.    It includes a set of methods that members of the scientific community agree will, if properly executed, provide valid and useful data.

8.  According to Kuhn, the social sciences differ from the natural sciences in that

    a.   social sciences lack an accepted paradigm upon which most members of
         the scientific community agree
    b.   although they have an accepted paradigm upon which most members of
         the scientific community agree, social scientists tend to align themselves
         with one of several different perspectives
    c.   there are a limited number of perspectives in the social sciences, whereas
         the number in the natural sciences seems unlimited
    d.   social sciences borrow perspectives from the natural sciences, whereas the
         natural sciences never borrow from the social sciences

9.  The relation between conscious awareness and unconscious mental forces can be
    considered analogous to the visible tip of an iceberg and the vast, submerged
    hulk that lies out of sight beneath the water. This notion best fits with which of
    the following perspectives?

    a.   psychodynamic
    b.   behaviorist
    c.   cognitive
    d.   evolutionary

10. Which of the following research methods is most associated with the
    psychodynamic perspective?

    a.   experimentation
    b.   introspection
    c.   case study
    d.   all of the above

11. The notion that the mind at birth can be considered a "tabula rasa" is
    attributable to

    a.   John Locke
    b.   Margaret Mead
    c.   Paul Broca
    d.   Rene Descartes

12. The notion of the mind as a "black box" is associated with which of the
    following views?

    a.   information processing
    b.   sociobiology
    c.   cross-cultural
    d.   behavioral

13.    Behaviorists do not believe that we can scientifically study unconscious motives. All of the following <u>except</u> one are problems that to behaviorists preclude the study of unconscious motives

    a.    They cannot be observed.
    b.    Only conscious thoughts can be studied according to the behaviorist approach.
    c.    They cannot be reliably measured.
    d.    Prediction and hypothesis-testing are impossible with such subject matter.

14.    The primary method of the behaviorist approach is

    a.    introspection
    b.    deduction
    c.    determinism
    d.    experimentation

15.    The notion of "information processing" is most associated with which perspective?

    a.    evolutionary        b.    Gestalt
    c.    cognitive           d.    behaviorist

16.    The primary method of the cognitive perspective is

    a.    introspection
    b.    deduction
    c.    case study
    d.    experimentation

17.    The field of study that is most concerned with the biological and evolutionary significance of animal behavior is

    a.    sociobiology
    b.    ethology
    c.    psychological anthropology
    d.    cross-cultural psychology

18.    Many, if not most, psychological processes

    a.    are predominantly attributable to environmental influences
    b.    are determined by innate, biological processes
    c.    reflect an interaction between nature and nurture
    d.    are primarily learned, and not biologically ordained

19.    A psychologist who accepts the behaviorist position that learning is the basis of behavior, but who also emphasizes the role of mental processes in determining the way individuals react to their environment could be called a(n)

       a.    evolutionary psychologist
       b.    sociobiologist
       c.    rationalist
       d.    cognitive-behaviorist

20.    Psychologists interested in such phenomena as prejudice, mob violence, and how people process information about themselves would most likely be classified as _____ psychologists.

       a.    clinical
       b.    health
       c.    industrial/organizational
       d.    social

# ANSWERS

## FILL-IN EXERCISES

1. nature-nurture  2. tabula rasa  3. unconscious  4. case study  5. stimuli
6. structuralism  7. father; introspection   8. experimental  9. black box  10. learned;
environmental  11. increase (reinforce); decrease (punish)  12. information processing
13. more  14. experimental  15. reproductive  16. adaptive  17. niche  18. innate
19. empiricist  20. social psychology

## APPLICATION

1.  Evolutionary perspective  2.  Behaviorist perspective  3.  Cognitive perspective
4.  Psychodynamic perspective

## SAMPLE TEST QUESTIONS

| | | | |
|---|---|---|---|
| 1. | d | 11. | a |
| 2. | d | 12. | d |
| 3. | a | 13. | b |
| 4. | c | 14. | d |
| 5. | c | 15. | c |
| 6. | c | 16. | d |
| 7. | a | 17. | b |
| 8. | a | 18. | c |
| 9. | a | 19. | d |
| 10. | c | 20. | d |

# Chapter 2
# RESEARCH METHODS IN PSYCHOLOGY

**PART ONE:** **PRE-READ AND WORK**
**OUTLINE AND LEARNING OBJECTIVES**

Pre-read this chapter's table of contents and end-of-chapter summary. Then, use the outline segment-by-segment to help you work through the chapter. Jot down your own questions, comments, and notes in the space provided. Make a note of key terms and of difficult areas that you will need to review (include page numbers). Then, answer the questions in the learning objectives section that follows. Check off those you are confident that you can answer well. Re-read the material in the text for the questions about which you are less confident. Record the important points from your reading in the space below each question.

## OUTLINE

I.   CHARACTERISTICS OF GOOD PSYCHOLOGICAL RESEARCH

A. Theoretical Framework

B. Standardized Procedures

C. Generalizability from a Sample

D. Objective Measurement

II.   EXPERIMENTAL RESEARCH

A. Step 1: Framing a Hypothesis

B. Step 2: Operationalizing Variables

C. Step 3: Developing a Standardized Procedure

D. Step 4: Selecting and Assigning Participants

E. Step 5: Applying Statistical Techniques to the Data

F. Step 6: Drawing Conclusions

G. Limitations of Experimental Research

III.  DESCRIPTIVE RESEARCH

A. Case Study Methods

B. Naturalistic Observation

C. Survey Research

IV.   CORRELATIONAL RESEARCH

A. **From Mind to Brain:** Researching the Brain

B. **A Global Vista:** Cross-Cultural Research

V.   HOW TO EVALUATE A STUDY CRITICALLY

A. Does the Theoretical Framework Make Sense?

B. Is the Sample Adequate and Appropriate?

C. Were the Measures and Procedures Adequate?

D. Are the Data Conclusive?

E. Are the Broader Conclusions Warranted?

## LEARNING OBJECTIVES

Upon completion of Chapter 2, you should be able to answer the following questions.

1.    What are a theory, a hypothesis, and a variable? How are they related to one another?

2.    What are the four characteristics of good psychological research?

3.    Differentiate between the internal and external validity of a study.

4.    What is meant by the "reliability" of a measure? Discuss three important kinds of reliability.

5.   Why are multiple measures important to obtain an accurate assessment of a variable?

6.   How do experimental methods allow researchers to assess cause-and-effect relations between variables?

7.   How do independent and dependent variables differ?

8.   What are the six steps involved in conceiving and executing an experiment?

9.   What is involved in "operationalizing" a variable?

10.  Why are control groups important in experimental research?

11.  What is the purpose of blind studies in experimental research? How do double-blind studies differ from single-blind studies?

12.  Why is random assignment important in experimental research?

13.  What are three limitations of experimental research?

14.  What is a quasi-experimental design? Why do researchers employ such a design?

15. What are the uses and limitations of each of the following descriptive methods?

   Case study

   Naturalistic observation

   Survey research

16. By what means do researchers minimize observer effects in naturalistic observational studies?

17. How do researchers using the survey method ensure that their sample reflects the demographic characteristics of the population of interest?

18. How do correlation coefficients represent the relation between variables? What is the difference between positive and negative correlations?

19. What is meant by the phrase "correlation does not imply causation"?

20. Compare the following methods researchers use to study the brain:

   electroencephalogram (EEG)

   computerized axial tomography (CT-scan)

   magnetic resonance imaging (MRI)

   positron emission tomography (PET)

   functional magnetic resonance imaging (fMRI).

21. What difficulties do researchers face when trying to transport research from one culture to another?

22.    What are seven important criteria that can be used to evaluate a study critically?

23.    What four conditions must be met before deception can be used in a study?

24.    Discuss the ethical controversy concerning the use of animals in psychological research.

## PART TWO:     REVIEW AND LEARN
## KEY TERMS, FILL-IN EXERCISES, APPLICATION AND USING WHAT YOU HAVE LEARNED

Before doing the exercises below, review the information you learned in this chapter. Reread the work you did in part one of this study guide chapter, plus the interim summaries and end-of-chapter summary in your textbook. Review any problem areas. Once you feel comfortable with the material, do the following exercises without referring to your notes or textbook. If you have difficulty with a term or question, mark it and come back to it. When you have finished an exercise, go back to your notes and the textbook to find the answers to the questions that gave you difficulty. Finally, check your answers (key terms against the textbook and the rest against the answer key).

## KEY TERMS

Theory       _____

_____

Hypothesis _____

_____

Variable     _____

_____

Continuous variable _____

_____

Categorical variable_____

_____

Standardized procedures _____

_____

Population _____

_____

Sample _____

_____

Participants (or Subjects) _____

_____

Generalizability _____

_____

Internal validity _____

_____

External validity _____

_____

Reliability _____

_____

Test-retest reliability _____

_____

Internal consistency _____

_____

Inter-rater reliability _____

_____

Validity _____

_____

Validation _____

_____

Multiple measures _____

_____

Error _____

_____

Experimental research _____

_____

Independent variable _____

_____

Dependent variable _____

_____

Operationalizing _____

_____

Control group _____

_____

Demand characteristics _____

_____

Blind studies _____

_____

Placebo effects _____

_____

Single-blind study _____

_____

Double-blind study _____

_____

Confounding variable _____

_____

Descriptive statistics _____

_____

Inferential statistics _____

_____

Quasi-experimental designs _____

_____

Descriptive research _____

_____

Case study _____

_____

Naturalistic observation _____

_____

Survey research _____

_____

Questionnaires _____

_____

Interviews _____

_____

Random sample _____

_____

Demographic characteristics _____

_____

Stratified random sample _____

_____

Correlational research _____

_____

Correlation coefficient _____

_____

Positive correlation _____

_____

Negative correlation _____

_____

Scatterplot graph _____

_____

Correlation matrix _____

_____

Electroencephalogram (EEG) _____

_____

Computerized axial tomography (CT-scan or CAT-scan) _____

_____

Magnetic resonance imaging (MRI) _____

_____

Positron emission tomography (PET) _____

_____

Functional magnetic resonance imaging (fMRI)_____

_____

## FILL-IN EXERCISES

Fill in the word or words that best fit in the spaces below.

1.  The individuals who take part in a study are referred to as _____.

2.  A variable that can be placed on a continuum is a _____ variable, whereas one comprised of groupings, classifications, or categories is a _____ variable.

3.  Researchers typically study the behavior of a particular group or subset of people in order to learn something about the larger _____.

4.  The term _____ refers to a measure's ability to produce consistent results.

5.    One advantage of experiments is that they can be _____, that is, repeated to see if the same findings emerge with a different sample.

6.    The ability of a measure to assess the variable it is supposed to measure is referred to as its _____.

7.    Because no psychological measure assesses a variable accurately 100% of the time, investigators often employ _____ measures of the variable.

8.    Turning an abstract concept into a concrete variable is called _____ the variable.

9.    To ensure that the only things that vary from participant to participant are the independent variables and the participants' performance on the dependent variables, investigators develop a _____ procedure for all participants.

10.    A double-blind study is a way of reducing the effects of the biases of both _____ and _____ .

11.    In analyzing the findings of a study, _____ statistics are used to summarize the essential features of the data in a table or graph, whereas _____ statistics are used to draw inferences from the sample studied to the population as a whole.

12.    Some psychologists argue that the aim of psychology should not be predicting behavior, but instead understanding the idiosyncratic personal meanings that lead to an individual's actions. Such psychologists take a _____, or interpretive stance on methodology.

13.    Using experimental methods allows researchers to directly assess _____-and-_____ relations between variables.

14.    The two most frequently used tools of survey researchers are _____ and _____.

15.    When using survey methods, sometimes proportional representation of different subpopulations is important to researchers. A _____ random sample specifies the percentage of participants to be drawn from each population category and then _____ selects from within each category.

## USING WHAT YOU HAVE LEARNED

In Chapter 2, you learned about different research methods that are used in psychology. Below you will find the names of various research methods. Identify which method best describes each of the examples of research studies that follow.

**Research Methods**

Naturalistic observation          Case study
Survey research                   Correlational research
Quasi-experiment                  Experiment

**Studies**

1.    The relation between college students' final exam grades and the number of hours they spent studying for the exam is examined.

2.    A psychology professor wants to determine whether showing videotapes as an adjunct to his lectures improves students' performance. He randomly creates two groups of students: those in one group watch videotapes that illustrate the material in the lecture, while those in the other just attend the lectures (no tapes). He then compares their grades on the exam.

3.    A researcher is interested in whether there are sex differences in grades in the Introduction to psychology course. She compares the grades of the female students to those of the male students in the course.

4.    Every term, the university asks students to complete a questionnaire evaluating the course they are taking and the professor who teaches it. The information is used to provide feedback to the department and to the professors concerning both course content and teaching methods.

5.    A team of developmental psychologists, interested in the phenomenon of bullying, spends several weeks observing children at recess and lunch break in their school playground.

6.    A clinical psychologist collects considerable information concerning each patient that she sees, including information concerning their childhood (family and school experiences), job and career, romantic relationships, and so on. Her goal is to put together a comprehensive picture of each patient.

## APPLICATION

### Situation

A researcher is interested in whether taking vitamin C has an effect on the number of colds people get.

### Questions to Answer

1.    If she wants to determine whether taking vitamin C actually reduces the number of colds people get (i.e., a cause-and-effect relationship), what type of research procedure should she use?

2.    What procedures would she follow in setting up such a study?

3.    What could she select for the independent and dependent variables?

4.    Do you think a control group would be important? Why? What kind of neutral condition could she use with a control group?

5.    How could she control for possible demand characteristics in the study?

## PART THREE:   TEST AND KNOW
## SAMPLE TEST QUESTIONS

Test how well you have learned this chapter's material by answering the sample test questions.  You may wish to mark your answers on a separate sheet of paper so you can reuse this test for exam review.  Once you have completed the exam, check your answers and then go back to your notes and the textbook to review questions you found difficult.

1.    Because case study research gains its insights from examining only one participant, generalization to a larger population is always uncertain. One way to minimize this limitation is to

   a.    use a multiple case study approach
   b.    avoid using the case study
   c.    employ experimental case study designs
   d.    stop trying to generalize

2.    The term _____ refers to the applicability of a study's findings to the entire population of interest to the researchers.

    a.    internal validity
    b.    generalizability
    c.    reliability
    d.    internal consistency

3.    A researcher is interested in whether watching "Sesame Street" on TV has a positive impact on children's grades at school. She records the number of days children watch "Sesame Street" over a one-month interval and relates it to their grades on their report cards at school. This study is best described as

    a.    experimental
    b.    quasi-experimental
    c.    a survey
    d.    correlational

4.    Turning an abstract concept into a concrete variable involves

    a.    operationalizing the variable
    b.    validating the variable
    c.    standardizing the variable
    d.    confounding the variable

5.    The major problem with survey methods is the following:

    a.    It is often difficult to get participants to participate in this kind of study.
    b.    People tend to describe their behaviors and attitudes in more flattering terms than others would use to describe them.
    c.    It is questionable whether the results can be generalized to the larger population.
    d.    It is often difficult to keep participants unaware of the purpose of the study and thus demand characteristics can be a major concern.

6.    In an experiment, the investigator can determine whether a _____ relation exists between two variables, whereas this cannot be determined in a study using correlational methods.

    a.    valid
    b.    cause-and-effect
    c.    generalizable
    d    reliable

7.  Assume an investigator has found a positive correlation between the number of aspirins people take and the number of headaches they get. The investigator could conclude the following from this correlation:

    a.  The number of aspirins taken and number of headaches suffered are related to one another.
    b.  People who take aspirin frequently seem to get fewer headaches.
    c.  Taking aspirin causes people to have fewer headaches.
    d.  Taking aspirin seems unrelated to whether people have headaches or not.

8.  A researcher has developed a new treatment for smoking which combines hypnosis and acupuncture. He randomly creates two groups of participants and administers his new treatment to one group, while the other group receives no treatment. He measures the number of cigarettes participants smoke in the 2 weeks following treatment. This study is best described as

    a.  descriptive
    b.  correlational
    c.  quasi-experimental
    d.  experimental

9.  What is the dependent variable in the above example?

    a.  the two groups of participants
    b.  the 2 weeks following treatment
    c.  hypnosis and acupuncture
    d.  the number of cigarettes smoked

10.  In the above example, it would be important for the researchers to ensure that participants are kept unaware of the goals of the research; otherwise, their behavior might be affected. To do so, the researcher would conduct

    a.  a single-blind study
    b.  a. quasi-experimental study
    c.  a case study
    d.  a demand characteristic

11.  In the above example, if participants in the treatment condition were older than those in the no-treatment condition, _____ would be a confounding variable.

    a.  smoking
    b.  the treatment
    c.  age
    d.  no treatment

12.    A hypothetical study of the relation between TV violence and aggressive behavior in children reveals a correlation of +.85 between the number of violent shows watched each week and children's level of aggressiveness. Based on these findings, which of the following conclusions might be true?

    a.    Watching violent TV leads to aggressive behavior in children.
    b.    Parents who do not allow their children to watch violent shows may discourage aggressive behavior in their children in other ways as well.
    c.    Children who are more aggressive may have more of a "taste" for violent shows than those who are less aggressive.
    d.    In fact, ALL of the above conclusions could be true.

13.    A correlation of zero means that

    a.    two variables are totally unrelated
    b.    as the first variable increases, the other decreases
    c.    as the first variable decreases, the other increases
    d.    participants tended to score around zero on both variables

14.    A procedure in which radioactive glucose is injected into the bloodstream allowing researchers to observe the brain in action is called

    a.    an electroencephalogram (EEG)
    b.    computerized axial tomography (CT scan)
    c.    magnetic resonance imaging (MRI)
    d.    positron emission tomography (PET)

15.    When deception is used in research, researchers must be sure to

    a.    pay the participants
    b.    debrief the participants afterward
    c.    instruct the participants not to talk about the true purposes of the study
    d.    ensure that participants do not deduce the true purpose of the study, which could cause demand characteristics to bias the results

16.    Experimental and quasi-experimental designs are useful in the context of _____, whereas case studies, naturalistic observation, and correlational studies are often more useful in the context of _____.

    a.    justification; discovery
    b.    discovery; justification
    c.    reliability; validation
    d.    validation; reliability

17. A systematic way to organize and explain observations, which includes a set of propositions or statements about the relations among various phenomena is a

   a. hypothesis
   b. paradigm
   c. theory
   d. model

18. If several ways of asking the same question yield similar results, a measure has

   a. test-retest reliability
   b. internal consistency
   c. inter-rater reliability
   d. internal validity

19. If the finding of a study can be generalized to situations outside the laboratory, the study has

   a. internal validity
   b. internal consistency
   c. external consistency
   d. external validity

20. The number that indicates the direction and strength of the relation between two variables is referred to as a

   a. correlation coefficient
   b. correlation matrix
   c. scatter plot
   d. correlation plot

# ANSWERS

## FILL-IN EXERCISES

1. participants (or subjects) 2. continuous; categorical 3. population 4. reliability
5. replicated 6. validity 7. multiple 8. operationalizing 9. standardized
10. participants; researchers 11. descriptive; inferential 12. hermeneutic 13. cause;
effect 14. questionnaires; interviews 15. stratified; randomly

## APPLICATION

1. Experimental research
2. Follow the six steps of conceiving and executing an experiment: frame hypothesis;
operationalize variables; develop standardized procedures; select and assign
participants to conditions; apply statistical techniques to the results; and draw
conclusions.
3. Independent variable -- level of vitamin C administered to each group
(e.g., 0 mg/day; 100 mg/day; 500 mg/day); Dependent variable -- number of colds
participants in each group report during the duration of the study.
4. Yes; because of placebo effects. Use a placebo control (e.g., an inert pill).
5. Use a blind study (single-blind to control for demand characteristics; double blind to
control as well for experimenter bias).

## USING WHAT YOU HAVE LEARNED

1. correlational research 2. experiment 3. quasi-experiment 4. survey research
5. naturalistic observation 6. case study

## SAMPLE TEST QUESTIONS

| 1. | a | 11. | c |
|----|---|-----|---|
| 2. | b | 12. | d |
| 3. | d | 13. | a |
| 4. | a | 14. | d |
| 5. | b | 15. | b |
| 6. | b | 16. | a |
| 7. | a | 17. | c |
| 8. | d | 18. | b |
| 9. | d | 19. | d |
| 10. | a | 20. | a |

# Chapter 2: Supplement
# STATISTICAL PRINCIPLES IN PSYCHOLOGICAL RESEARCH

**PART ONE:      PRE-READ AND WORK**
## OUTLINE AND LEARNING OBJECTIVES

Pre-read this chapter's table of contents and end-of-chapter summary. Then, use the outline segment-by-segment to help you work through the chapter. Jot down your own questions, comments, and notes in the space provided. Make a note of difficult areas that you will need to review (include page numbers). Then, answer the questions in the learning objectives section that follows. Check off those you are confident that you can answer well. Re-read the material in the text for the questions about which you are less confident. Record the important points from your reading in the space below each question.

## OUTLINE

I.     SUMMARIZING THE DATA: DESCRIPTIVE STATISTICS

    A. Measures of Central Tendency

    B. Variability

    C. The Normal Distribution

II.    TESTING THE HYPOTHESIS: INFERENTIAL STATISTICS

    A. Statistical Significance

B. Common Tests of Statistical Significance

## III.   SOME CONCLUDING THOUGHTS

## LEARNING OBJECTIVES

Upon completion of Chapter 2: Supplement, you should be able to answer the following questions..

1.      How do researchers chart a frequency distribution?

2.      What are the similarities and differences between the three most common measures of central tendency -- mean, mode, and median?

3.      What are two methods of measuring variability?

4.      What are the important characteristics of a normal distribution?

5.      Why are tests of statistical significance necessary?

6.      What is meant by the expression "p <.01?"

7.      What are two frequently used tests of statistical significance? When would it be appropriate to use one or the other?

8.    How do inferential statistics differ from descriptive statistics?

## PART TWO:    REVIEW AND LEARN
## KEY TERMS, FILL-IN EXERCISES, APPLICATION AND USING WHAT YOU HAVE LEARNED

Before doing the exercises below, review the information you learned in this chapter. Reread the work you did in part one of this study guide chapter, plus the interim summaries and end-of-chapter summary in your textbook. Review any problem areas. Once you feel comfortable with the material, do the following exercises without referring to your notes or textbook. If you have difficulty with a term or question, mark it and come back to it. When you have finished an exercise, go back to your notes and the textbook to find the answers to the questions that gave you difficulty. Finally, check your answers (key terms against the textbook and the rest against the answer key).

## KEY TERMS

Upon completion of Chapter 2: Supplement, you should be able to define the following terms.

Frequency distribution    _____

_____

Histogram    _____

_____

Measures of central tendency    _____

_____

Mean _____

_____

Mode _____

_____

Median _____

_____

Variability _____

_____

Range _____

_____

Standard deviation (SD) _____

_____

Normal distribution _____

_____

Percentile Scores _____

_____

Tests of statistical significance _____

_____

Probability value ($p$-value) _____

_____

Chi-square test _____

_____

t-test _____

_____

Analysis of variance (ANOVA) _____

_____

## APPLICATION

### Situation

A researcher is interested in whether there is a significant difference between science students and general arts students in amount of time spent studying. She administers a questionnaire that asks the number of hours spent studying over the past week to 15 science students and 15 general arts students. She collects the following results:

| **Science Students** | | **General Arts Students** | |
|---|---|---|---|
| Student # | Studying Hours | Student # | Studying Hours |
| 1 | 20 | 1 | 19 |
| 2 | 20 | 2 | 27 |
| 3 | 28 | 3 | 32 |
| 4 | 21 | 4 | 23 |
| 5 | 28 | 5 | 27 |
| 6 | 21 | 6 | 31 |
| 7 | 35 | 7 | 27 |
| 8 | 30 | 8 | 16 |
| 9 | 28 | 9 | 17 |
| 10 | 22 | 10 | 25 |
| 11 | 25 | 11 | 26 |
| 12 | 26 | 12 | 28 |
| 13 | 19 | 13 | 22 |
| 14 | 27 | 14 | 29 |
| 15 | 24 | 15 | 24 |

### Questions to Answer

1. Calculate the mean, median, and mode for each group of students.

2. Calculate the range of scores for each group.

3. What would be the appropriate test to assess whether there is a statistically significant difference between the two groups? What would be an acceptable $p$ value for the difference?

## FILL-IN EXERCISES

Fill in the word or words that best fit in the spaces below.

1.   A method of organizing the data to show how frequently subjects received each of the many possible scores is referred to as a _____ _____.

2.   The three most common measures of central tendency are the _____, the _____, and the _____.

3.   The simplest measure of variability is the _____ of scores.

4.   A _____-value represents the probability that the results obtained in a study were just a matter of chance.

5.   An analysis of variance would be the appropriate test of statistical significance if the _____ variable is continuous and the _____ variable is categorical.

## PART THREE:   TEST AND KNOW
## SAMPLE TEST QUESTIONS

Test how well you have learned this chapter's material by answering the sample test questions.  You may wish to mark your answers on a separate sheet of paper so you can reuse this test for exam review.  Once you have completed the exam, check your answers and then go back to your notes and the textbook to review questions you found difficult.

1.   The score that falls in the middle of a distribution of scores, with half the subjects scoring below it and half above it, is the

   a.   mean                            b.   mode
   c.   median                          d.   standard deviation

2.   A frequency distribution in which the ranges of scores are plotted along the X-axis and the frequency of scores in each range is plotted on the Y-axis is referred to as a

   a.   measure of central tendency     b.   bell-curve
   c.   normal distribution             d.   histogram

3.   A measure of variability that is more useful than the *range* is the

   a.   histogram                       b.   normal distribution
   c.   central tendency                d.   standard deviation

4.    In a(n) _____ _____, the scores of most subjects fall in the middle of the bell-shaped distribution, and progressively fewer subjects have scores at either extreme.

    a.    normal distribution         b.    standard deviation
    c.    inferential statistic          d.    frequency distribution

5.    Tests of statistical significance determine

    a.    whether the results of a study are high in practical significance
    b.    whether the results of a study are high in theoretical significance
    c.    whether the results of a study are likely to have occurred simply by chance
    d.    whether the results of a study apply to situations outside the lab in which the research took place

6.    By convention, psychologists accept the results of a study whenever the probability of findings attributable to chance is less than

    a.    50%        b.    10%        c.    5%        d.    1%

7.    The best way to ensure that the results of a study are not accidental is to

    a.    use a frequency distribution     b.    use a large sample of subjects.
    c.    use a normal distribution.         d.    use a chi-square test.

8.    If the independent variable is categorical, while the dependent variable is continuous, the most appropriate test of statistical significance would be a(n)

    a.    analysis of variance         b.    chi-squared test
    c.    standard deviation          d.    correlation

9.    The expression $p < .01$ means

    a.    the chances of the findings of this study being spurious are 1 in 100
    b.    there is a good chance that less than 100 subjects participated in this study
    c.    only 1 out of a sample of 100 likely participated in this study
    d.    the results of this study apply only to 1 in 100 individuals

10.    The statistical test that compares observed data with data that would be expected by chance and tests the likelihood that the differences between observed and expected are accidental is a(n)

    a.    analysis of variance         b.    chi-squared test.
    c.    t-test.          d.    a correlation

# ANSWERS

## FILL-IN EXERCISES

1. frequency distribution  2. mean, mode, median  3. range  4. $p$ (or probability)
5. dependent; independent

## APPLICATION

| 1. | | Science Students | Arts Students |
|----|----|----|----|
| | mean | 24.93 | 24.87 |
| | median | 25 | 26 |
| | mode | 28 | 27 |
| 2. | range | 16 | 16 |

3.    t-test;  p<.05

## SAMPLE TEST QUESTIONS

1.    c
2.    d
3.    d
4.    a
5.    c
6.    c
7.    b
8.    a
9.    a
10.    b

# Chapter 3
# BIOLOGICAL BASES OF MENTAL LIFE AND BEHAVIOR

## PART ONE: PRE-READ AND WORK
## OUTLINE AND LEARNING OBJECTIVES

Pre-read this chapter's table of contents and end-of-chapter summary. Then, use the outline segment-by-segment to help you work through the chapter. Jot down your own questions, comments, and notes in the space provided. Make a note of key terms and of difficult areas that you will need to review (include page numbers). Then, answer the questions in the learning objectives section that follows. Check off those you are confident that you can answer well. Re-read the material in the text for the questions about which you are less confident. Record the important points from your reading in the space below each question.

## OUTLINE

I. NEURONS: BASIC UNITS OF THE NERVOUS SYSTEM

   A. Anatomy of a Neuron

   B. Firing of a Neuron

   C. Transmission of Information Between Cells

II. THE ENDOCRINE SYSTEM

III.    THE PERIPHERAL NERVOUS SYSTEM

A. The Somatic Nervous System

B. The Autonomic Nervous System

IV.    THE CENTRAL NERVOUS SYSTEM

A. Evolution of the Central Nervous System

B. The Spinal Cord

C. The Hindbrain

D. **One Step Further:** Tracking Down the Functions of the Cerebellum

E. The Midbrain

F. The Forebrain

G. The Cerebral Cortex

H. **From Mind to Brain:** The Impact of Frontal and Temporal Lobe Damage on Personality

I. **A Global Vista:** Environment, Culture, and the Brain

## V.     MIND, BRAIN, AND GENE

A. Genetics

B. Behavioral Genetics

## VI.     SOME CONCLUDING THOUGHTS

## LEARNING OBJECTIVES

Upon completion of Chapter 3, you should be able to answer the following questions.

1.     Differentiate between three kinds of neurons.

2.     What are the functions of the dendrites and the axon?

3.    Why is myelination important for the transmission of nerve impulses?

4.    How do graded potentials differ from action potentials?

5.    How are sodium and potassium ions involved in the transmission of an impulse down the axon?

6.    How do neurons communicate chemically with other neurons?

7.    How do excitatory and inhibitory neurotransmitters differ?

8.    What are the psychological functions of the following neurotransmitters?

Glutamate

Gamma aminobutyric acid (GABA)

Dopamine

Serotonin

Acetylcholine (Ach)

9.    What is Parkinson's disease and what role does dopamine play in this disease?

10.    What are the functions of the following endocrine glands?

Pituitary

Thyroid

Adrenal

Pancreas

Gonads

11.    In what ways do the functions of the sympathetic nervous system and the parasympathetic nervous system differ?

12.    How do antianxiety medications block the action of neurotransmitters involved in sympathetic arousal?

13.    What is the major function of each of the following areas of the brain?

Medulla oblongata

Cerebellum

Reticular formation

Hypothalamus

Thalamus

Septal area

Amygdala

Hippocampus

Basal ganglia

14.    What are three functions performed by the cerebral cortex?

15.    How do the functions of the primary and association areas of the cortex differ?

16.    What are the functions of the following four lobes of each hemisphere?

Occipital

Parietal

Frontal

Temporal

17.    How is space allocated to different parts of the body in the motor and somatosensory cortexes?

18.    What are the results of damage to Broca's and Wernicke's areas?

19.    Describe the personality changes that are consequences of damage to the frontal and temporal lobes.

20.    What is meant by cerebral lateralization? List the various functions for which the left and right hemisphere are dominant.

21.    How does split-brain research provide evidence for cerebral lateralization?

22.    Describe the cognitive and/or motor differences that have been found between females and males. What are the biological and cultural explanations for these differences?

23.    How are the genes from each parent transmitted to their children?

24.    How do researchers assess the heritability of various characteristics?

## PART TWO:     REVIEW AND LEARN
## KEY TERMS, FILL-IN EXERCISES, APPLICATION AND USING WHAT YOU HAVE LEARNED

Before doing the exercises below, review the information you learned in this chapter. Reread the work you did in part one of this study guide chapter, plus the interim summaries and end-of-chapter summary in your textbook. Review any problem areas. Once you feel comfortable with the material, do the following exercises without referring to your notes or textbook. If you have difficulty with a term or question, mark it and come back to it. When you have finished an exercise, go back to your notes and the textbook to find the answers to the questions that gave you difficulty. Finally, check your answers (key terms against the textbook and the rest against the answer key).

## KEY TERMS

Neurons _____

_____

Sensory neurons (afferent neurons) _____

_____

Motor neurons (efferent neurons) _____

_____

Interneurons _____

_____

Cell body (or soma) _____

_____

Dendrites _____

_____

Axon _____

_____

Collateral branches _____

_____

Myelin sheath        _____

_____

Nodes of Ranvier     _____

_____

Terminal buttons     _____

_____

Synapses             _____

_____

Synaptic cleft       _____

_____

Resting potential    _____

_____

Depolarization       _____

_____

Hyperpolarization    _____

_____

Graded potentials    _____

_____

Action potential     _____

_____

Presynaptic neuron _____

_____

Postsynaptic neuron    _____

_____

Synaptic vesicles    _____

_____

Neurotransmitters    _____

_____

Receptors    _____

_____

Excitatory neurotransmitter    _____

_____

Inhibitory neurotransmitter    _____

_____

Epinephrine and norepinephrine    _____

_____

Endorphins    _____

_____

Glutamate    _____

_____

GABA    _____

_____

Dopamine _____

_____

Parkinson's disease _____

_____

Serotonin _____

_____

Acetylcholine (Ach) _____

_____

Endocrine system _____

_____

Hormone _____

_____

Adrenaline _____

_____

Noradrenaline _____

_____

Pituitary gland _____

_____

Thyroid gland _____

_____

Hypothyroidism _____

_____

Adrenal glands _____

_____

Pancreas _____

_____

Gonads _____

_____

Testes _____

_____

Testosterone _____

_____

Ovaries _____

_____

Estrogens _____

_____

Peripheral nervous system (PNS) _____

_____

Somatic nervous system _____

_____

Autonomic nervous system (ANS) _____

_____

Sympathetic nervous system _____

_____

Parasympathetic nervous system _____

_____

Central nervous system (CNS) _____

_____

Spinal cord _____

_____

Spinal nerves _____

_____

Nerves _____

_____

Tracts _____

_____

Hindbrain _____

_____

Medulla oblongata _____

_____

Cerebellum _____

_____

Reticular formation _____

_____

Midbrain _____

_____

Tectum     _____

_____

Tegmentum  _____

_____

Forebrain  _____

_____

Hypothalamus  _____

_____

Thalamus   _____

_____

Limbic system  _____

_____

Septal area  _____

_____

Amygdala   _____

_____

Hippocampus  _____

_____

Basal ganglia_____

_____

Cerebral cortex  _____

_____

Gyri _____

_____

Sulci _____

_____

Primary areas _____

_____

Association areas _____

_____

Cerebral hemispheres _____

_____

Longitudinal fissure _____

_____

Corpus callosum _____

_____

Occipital lobes _____

_____

Polysensory areas _____

_____

Parietal lobes_____

_____

Somatosensory cortex _____

_____

Central fissure _____

_____

Frontal lobes _____

_____

Motor cortex _____

_____

Broca's area _____

_____

Broca's aphasia _____

_____

Temporal lobes _____

_____

Wernicke's area _____

_____

Wernicke's aphasia _____

_____

Cerebral lateralization _____

_____

Split-brain _____

_____

Phenotypes _____

_____

Genotypes _____

_____

Gene _____

_____

Chromosomes _____

_____

Monozygotic (MZ) twins _____

_____

Dizygotic (DZ) twins _____

_____

Behavioral genetics _____

_____

Heritability coefficient _____

_____

## FILL-IN EXERCISES

Fill in the word or words that best fit in the spaces below.

1.      _____ neurons carry sensory information to the spinal cord, which then relays the information to the brain. _____ neurons transmit commands from the brain to the glands and musculature of the body.

2.      Branch-like extensions of the neuron, called _____, receive information from other neurons. If a neuron receives enough stimulation, it passes information to other neurons through its _____.

3.      The _____ matter of the brain is composed of myelinated _____.

4.      Multiple sclerosis is a disease in which the _____ _____ on large clusters of neurons degenerates, causing jerky, uncoordinated movement.

5.  The hormone adrenaline is the same compound as the neurotransmitter _____.

6.  The male gonads, referred to as _____, produce the hormone _____. The female gonads, referred to as _____, produce the hormone _____.

7.  The somatic nervous system, because it is involved in intentional actions, is also called the _____ nervous system.

8.  The _____ comprises 80% of the human brain's volume.

9.  Damage to the _____ _____ is a major cause of coma.

10. The hills and valleys making up the convolutions of the cortex are referred to as _____ and _____, respectively.

11. The _____ areas of the cortex receive direct sensory information or initiate motor movements, while the _____ areas are involved in constructing perceptions, ideas, and plans.

12. _____ are abnormal tissue growths in the brain that may put pressure on brain structures and destroy existing cells.

13. _____ twins develop from the union of the same sperm and egg.


## APPLICATION

In each of the following hypothetical examples, an individual has suffered an injury to some area of the brain. Try to determine, from what you've read in Chapter 3, where the injury may be.

1.  Following neurosurgery to control life-threatening seizures, a patient is unable to remember new information. You have interviewed this patient on several occasions, yet every time you meet with her, she introduces herself anew to you.

2.  A former boxer displays symptoms similar to someone who is inebriated. His speech is slurred and his balance is affected, so that he staggers when he walks.

3.  Following a car accident in which her head violently struck the dashboard, a patient reports difficulty motivating herself and cannot seem to get started on any task. She has become quiet and withdrawn, preferring to spend her time alone, doing nothing.

4.    Following a stroke, a patient is unable to comprehend spoken language. She does attempt to speak, and her speech has normal rhythm and fluency; however, what comes out is not very comprehensible.

## USING WHAT YOU HAVE LEARNED

In Chapter 3, the sympathetic nervous system was described as an emergency system that is typically activated in response to threats to the organism. Its job is to ready the body for fight or flight, and it does so in several ways. Anxiety and panic attacks were described as the result of such sympathetic activity, where the autonomic nervous system may over-react to an event in the environment.

Think back to a situation in which you recently experienced anxiety. It may have been a situation where you had to speak before a group of people. Maybe it involved writing an examination. Or maybe it was flying or riding in a fast moving elevator.

1.    What kind of physical sensations did you experience?

2.    Can you see how those sensations reflect the functioning of the sympathetic nervous system?

3.    Can you see the potentially adaptive role those sensations might have, had you been experiencing real physical threat?

4.    Think of the role the adrenal glands play in such a situation. Can you remember feeling aroused and jittery for some time even after the event had passed because of the higher levels of adrenaline in your blood?

## PART THREE:   TEST AND KNOW
## SAMPLE TEST QUESTIONS

Test how well you have learned this chapter's material by answering the sample test questions.  You may wish to mark your answers on a separate sheet of paper so you can reuse this test for exam review.  Once you have completed the exam, check your answers and then go back to your notes and the textbook to review questions you found difficult.

1.    The nervous system is comprised of three types of neurons:

   a.    sensory neurons, motor neurons, and interneurons
   b.    sensory neurons, afferent neurons, and interneurons
   c.    sensory neurons, afferent neurons, and efferent neurons
   d.    sensory neurons, motor neurons, and efferent neurons

2.    The "gray matter" of the brain gets its color from

    a.    myelinated axons
    b.    cell bodies, dendrites, and unmyelinated axons
    c.    synapses
    d.    myelinated cell bodies and dendrites

3.    Connections between neurons occur at what are called

    a.    terminal buttons
    b.    nodes of Ranvier
    c.    soma
    d.    synapses

4.    Some people respond to MSG in Chinese food with neurological symptoms such as tingling and numbing, because the ingredient activates _____ receptors in their brains.

    a.    glutamate          b.    GABA
    c.    dopamine        d.    acetylcholine

5.    The neurotransmitter involved in sleep, emotional arousal, aggression, and pain regulation is

    a.    dopamine
    b.    serotonin
    c.    acetylcholine
    d.    endorphin

6.    Parkinson's disease results from degeneration of the _____-releasing cells of the substantia nigra.

    a.    dopamine
    b.    serotonin
    c.    acetylcholine
    d.    endorphin

7.    The endocrine gland(s) that is (are) more directly connected to the CNS than any other endocrine gland is (are) the

    a.    thyroid gland
    b.    adrenal glands
    c.    pituitary gland
    d.    gonads

8.    The nervous system that prepares the body for fighting or fleeing in response to threats is the

    a.    sympathetic nervous system
    b.    parasympathetic nervous system
    c.    somatic nervous system
    d.    peripheral nervous system

9.    Sexual activity is a good example of the delicate balance between

    a.    the central and peripheral nervous systems.
    b.    the somatic and autonomic nervous systems.
    c.    the afferent and efferent nervous systems.
    d.    the sympathetic and parasympathetic nervous systems.

10.   The area of the primitive brain specialized for equilibrium and balance is the

    a.    brainstem                    b.    forebrain
    c.    midbrain                     d.    hindbrain

11.   One of the most important functions of the hypothalamus is

    a.    relaying sensory information to higher brain centers
    b.    maintaining consciousness and regulating activity states
    c.    maintaining homeostasis
    d.    coordinating smooth, well-sequenced movements

12.   The area of the brainstem responsible for maintaining consciousness and regulating activity states is the

    a.    medulla oblongata           b.    cerebellum
    c.    reticular formation          d.    thalamus

13.   The subcortical cerebral structure that is especially involved in learning and remembering emotionally significant events is the

    a.    amygdala                     b.    hippocampus
    c.    septal area                  d.    basal ganglia

14.   The occipital lobes are involved in

    a.    the sense of touch and the experience of one's own body in space.
    b.    visual sensation and perception.
    c.    attention, planning, abstract thinking, and social skills.
    d.    auditory sensation and perception and language.

15.   A brain-injured patient appears callous, grandiose, and boastful, and tends to make tactless comments. The area of the brain that is most likely damaged is the

   a.   frontal lobes            b.   parietal lobes
   c.   occipital lobes          d.   temporal lobes

16.   In most people, the right hemisphere is dominant for

   a.   language
   b.   logic
   c.   analytical thinking
   d.   recognition of faces and places

17.   On the average, males score higher than females on tests of

   a.   spatial processing
   b.   verbal fluency
   c.   perceptual speed
   d.   manual dexterity

18.   Which type of twins share as much with each other, in terms of degree of relatedness, as they do with each of their parents?

   a.   monozygotic twins
   b.   dizygotic twins
   c.   trizygotic twins
   d.   identical twins

19.   "Heritability" connotes the degree to which

   a.   variability in an observed characteristic can be accounted for by genetic variability
   b.   a trait is genetically determined
   c.   various relatives share genetic material
   d.   MZ twins and DZ twins differ on a particular trait

20.   Psychologists interested in genetics study the way observable psychological characteristics, referred to as _____, reflect underlying genetic blueprints, which are called _____.

   a.   genotypes; phenotypes
   b.   chromosomes; genes
   c.   phenotypes, genotypes
   d.   heritability coefficients; degree of relatedness

# ANSWERS

## FILL-IN EXERCISES

1. afferent (sensory); efferent (motor)  2. dendrites; axon  3. white; axons  4. myelin sheath  5. epinephrine  6. testes, testosterone; ovaries, estrogen  7. voluntary  8. cortex  9. reticular formation  10. gyri; sulci  11. primary; association  12. tumors  13. monozygotic

## APPLICATION

1. hippocampus  2. cerebellum  3. frontal lobes  4. Wernicke's area

## SAMPLE TEST QUESTIONS

| | | | |
|---|---|---|---|
| 1. | a | 11. | c |
| 2. | b | 12. | c |
| 3. | d | 13. | a |
| 4. | a | 14. | b |
| 5. | b | 15. | a |
| 6. | a | 16. | d |
| 7. | c | 17. | a |
| 8. | a | 18. | b |
| 9. | d | 19. | a |
| 10. | d | 20. | c |

# Chapter 4
# SENSATION AND PERCEPTION

PART ONE:    PRE-READ AND WORK
OUTLINE AND LEARNING OBJECTIVES

Pre-read this chapter's table of contents and end-of-chapter summary.  Then, use the outline segment-by-segment to help you work through the chapter. Jot down your own questions, comments, and notes in the space provided. Make a note of key terms and of difficult areas that you will need to review (include page numbers). Then, answer the questions in the learning objectives section that follows. Check off those you are confident that you can answer well. Re-read the material in the text for the questions about which you are less confident. Record the important points from your reading in the space below each question.

## OUTLINE

I.    BASIC PRINCIPLES

II.    SENSING THE ENVIRONMENT

A. Transduction

B. Absolute Thresholds

C. **One Step Further:** Signal Detection

D. Difference Thresholds

E. Sensory Adaptation

## III.    Vision

A. The Nature of Light

B. The Eye

C. Neural Pathways

D. Perceiving in Color

## IV.    Hearing

A. The Nature of Sound

B. The Ear

C. Neural Pathways

V.   OTHER SENSES

    A. Smell

    B. Taste

    C. Skin Senses

    D. **From Mind to Brain:** Personality and Pain

    E. Proprioceptive Senses

VI.   PERCEPTION

    A. Organizing Sensory Experience

    B. **A Global Vista:** Culture and Perceptual Illusions

    C. Interpreting Sensory Experience

## VII.  SOME CONCLUDING THOUGHTS

## LEARNING OBJECTIVES

Upon completion of Chapter 4, you should be able to answer the following questions.

1.    How does perception differ from sensation?

2.    What three general principles underlie the processes of sensation and perception?

3.    Discuss the following five features that are common to all sensory modalities:

      Transduction

      Absolute threshold

      Signal detection

      Difference threshold

      Sensory adaptation

4.    What is Weber's law?  Fechner's law? Stevens's power law? What are the strengths and weaknesses of each?

5.    Describe the path light travels as it enters the eye and is focused on the retina.

6.    How do photoreceptors transform light into sight?

7.   Describe the neural pathway followed by impulses from the optic nerve to the visual cortex.

8.   Describe the trichromatic theory of color.

9.   How does the opponent-process theory of color derivation explain afterimages?

10.   What is the difference between the acoustic energy properties of frequency, complexity, and amplitude?

11.   What are the roles of the outer, middle, and inner ear in the process of hearing?

12.   How do place theory and frequency theory, together, explain the experiences of pitch and loudness?

13.   Describe the neural pathway followed by impulses from the auditory nerve to the auditory cortex.

14.   How is information from the ears integrated in the process of sound localization?

15.   Describe the path to the brain followed by information from the smell receptors and taste receptors.

16.   What are the three qualities that constitute the sense of touch?

17.    What is phantom limb pain? How does gate-control theory account for this phenomenon?

18.    How are chronic pain and personality style related?

19.    Describe two proprioceptive senses -- kinesthesia and the vestibular sense.

20.    Distinguish among the following four aspects of perceptual organization: form perception, depth perception, movement perception, and perceptual constancy.

21.    What are the six basic perceptual rules, according to Gestalt psychologists, that the brain follows as it organizes sensory input into meaningful wholes?

22.    What is Biederman's *recognition by components* theory? How would it explain channel surfing?

23.    How do binocular cues differ from monocular cues? How do these types of cues provide information about depth and distance?

24.    What are two systems that appear involved in motion perception?

25.    How is size constancy involved in the Müller-Lyer illusion and the Ponzo illusion? In what ways do culture and experience affect susceptibility to these illusions?

26.    How can bottom-up and top-down processing be viewed as complementary approaches?


27.    How do context and schemas influence the interpretation of experience?


## PART TWO:    REVIEW AND LEARN
## KEY TERMS, FILL-IN EXERCISES, APPLICATION AND USING WHAT YOU HAVE LEARNED

Before doing the exercises below, review the information you learned in this chapter. Reread the work you did in part one of this study guide chapter, plus the interim summaries and end-of-chapter summary in your textbook.  Review any problem areas.  Once you feel comfortable with the material, do the following exercises without referring to your notes or textbook.  If you have difficulty with a term or question, mark it and come back to it.  When you have finished an exercise, go back to your notes and the textbook to find the answers to the questions that gave you difficulty.  Finally, check your answers (key terms against the textbook and the rest against the answer key).

## KEY TERMS

Sensation    _____

_____

Perception    _____

_____

Psychophysics    _____

_____

Echolocation _____

_____

Receptors _____

_____

Transduction_____

_____

Doctrine of specific nerve energies _____

_____

Absolute threshold _____

_____

Signal detection theory _____

_____

Response bias (or decision criterion) _____

_____

Difference threshold (just noticeable difference) _____

_____

Weber's law _____

_____

Fechner's law _____

_____

Stevens's power law _____

_____

Sensory adaptation _____

_____

Cornea  _____

_____

Iris  _____

_____

Pupil  _____

_____

Lens  _____

_____

Accommodation  _____

_____

Retina_____

_____

Visual acuity _____

_____

Nearsightedness (myopia) _____

_____

Farsightedness (hyperopia)  _____

_____

Photoreceptors  _____

_____

Rods  _____

_____

Cones _____

_____

Bipolar cells _____

_____

Ganglion cells _____

_____

Optic nerve _____

_____

Fovea _____

_____

Optic disk (blind spot) _____

_____

Bleaching_____

_____

Dark adaptation _____

_____

Light adaptation _____

_____

Receptive fields _____

_____

Optic chiasm_____

_____

Superior colliculus _____

_____

Lateral geniculate nucleus _____

_____

Blindsight _____

_____

Feature detectors _____

_____

Simple cells _____

_____

Complex cells _____

_____

Hypercomplex cells _____

_____

"What" pathway _____

_____

"Where" pathway _____

_____

Hue _____

_____

Saturation _____

_____

Lightness _____

_____

Young-Helmholtz (trichromatic) theory _____

_____

Subtractive color mixture _____

_____

Additive color mixture _____

_____

Afterimages _____

_____

Opponent-process theory _____

_____

Color-opponent cells _____

_____

Audition _____

_____

Cycle _____

_____

Frequency _____

_____

Amplitude _____

_____

Complexity _____

_____

Pinna _____

_____

Auditory canal _____

_____

Eardrum (tympanic membrane) _____

_____

Cochlea _____

_____

Ossicles _____

_____

Basilar membrane _____

_____

Hair cells _____

_____

Tectorial membrane_____

_____

Auditory nerve _____

_____

Place theory _____

_____

Frequency theory    _____

_____

Binaural neurons    _____

_____

Olfaction    _____

_____

Pheromones _____

_____

Olfactory epithelium    _____

_____

Olfactory bulb    _____

_____

Olfactory nerve    _____

_____

Gustation    _____

_____

Taste buds    _____

_____

Papillae    _____

_____

Substance P    _____

_____

Phantom limb pain _____

_____

Gate-control theory _____

_____

Proprioceptive senses    _____

_____

Vestibular sense    _____

_____

Vestibular sacs    _____

_____

Semicircular canals _____

_____

Kinesthesia    _____

_____

Perceptual organization    _____

_____

Form perception    _____

_____

Gestalt psychologists    _____

_____

Figure-ground perception _____

_____

Similarity _____

_____

Proximity _____

_____

Good continuation _____

_____

Simplicity _____

_____

Closure _____

_____

Recognition-by-components _____

_____

Perceptual illusions _____

_____

Depth perception _____

_____

Binocular visual cues _____

_____

Retinal disparity _____

_____

Monocular visual cues _____

_____

Motion perception _____

_____

Motion detectors _____

_____

Perceptual constancy _____

_____

Convergence _____

_____

Perceptual interpretation _____

_____

Direct perception _____

_____

Visual cliff _____

_____

Bottom-up processing _____

_____

Top-down processing _____

_____

Perceptual set _____

_____

Schemas _____

_____

## FILL-IN EXERCISES

Fill in the word or words that best fit in the spaces below.

1.      _____ are immediate experiences of qualities (such as red or hot), whereas _____ are always experiences of objects or events.

2.      The minimal amount of physical energy needed for an observer to notice a stimulus is called an _____ _____.

3.      The world as subjectively experienced by an individual, referred to as the _____ world, is a joint product of external reality and the person's creative efforts to understand and depict it mentally.

4.      The _____ _____ is the lowest level of stimulation required to sense that a change in stimulation has occurred.

5.      _____ _____ law states that as the perceived intensity of a stimulus grows arithmetically, the actual magnitude of the stimulus grows exponentially.

6.      The innermost layer of the retina contains two types of photoreceptors: _____ which are specialized for color vision, and _____ which produce images in black, white, and gray, only.

7.      Hubel and Wisel discovered _____ _____ in the cortex, specialized neurons that fire only when stimulation in their receptive field matches a particular pattern or orientation.

8.      The three psychological dimensions of color are _____, _____, and _____.

9.      Young adults can hear frequencies from about _____ to about _____ Hertz (Hz), though, as with most senses, capacity diminishes with age.

10.     The process of hearing begins in the _____ ear, where sound waves are funneled into the ear by the _____, the skin-covered cartilage that protrudes from the sides of the head.

11.     Failure of the outer or middle ear to conduct sound to the receptors in the hair cells is called _____ loss. Failure of receptors in the inner ear or in any auditory pathway in the brain is called _____ loss.

12.     The four basic tastes are _____, _____, _____, and _____.

13. Transduction of taste occurs in the _____ _____, most of which are located on the bumps on the surface of the tongue, called _____.

14. Sensitivity to pressure varies considerably over the surface of the body. The most sensitive regions are the _____ and _____, and the least sensitive are the _____ and _____.

15. Of all of the senses, _____ is probably the most affected by beliefs, expectations, and emotional states.

16. Aside from the five traditional senses -- vision, hearing, smell, taste, and touch -- two additional senses, namely _____ and the _____ sense, provide information about the body's position and movement.

17. _____ _____ refers to the organization of sensations into meaningful shapes and patterns.

18. The monocular cue of _____ occurs when one object blocks part of another, leading to perception of the occluded object as more distant.

19. The visual perception of movement begins in the retina itself, with ganglion cells called _____ _____ that are particularly sensitive to movement.

20. Generating meaning from sensory experience is the task of _____ _____.

21. Experience with the environment shapes perceptual interpretation by creating perceptual expectations, called _____ _____.


## USING WHAT YOU HAVE LEARNED

Having just studied the topics of sensation and perception, you likely have a great deal of new insight into a number of "real life" questions that puzzle a lot of people. Based on what you have read, address each of the following questions.

1. When the lights come on in the theater at the end of a movie, why do they seem so much brighter than when you first entered the theater before the movie started?

2. Does an X-ray of your leg actually look different to a radiologist than to the average person?

3.    When you first walk into a crowded room, why does the noise seem unbearable, but after a few minutes, you hardly even notice it?

4.    Why can your dog hear a "silent" dog whistle, while you can't?

5.    Is grass really green, to a cow?

6.    How are blind people able to read the raised dots that constitute Braille?

7.    Why is it that whenever you have a head-cold and cannot smell because of your stuffy nose, all the food you eat tastes bland?

8.    Why does a needle seem to hurt less when the doctor distracts you by talking or telling a joke?

9.    How is it that you can see colored images on your color television?

10.   Why does your singing sound so much better in the shower compared with how it sounds out of the shower?

## APPLICATION

**Situation**

You've been lucky to land a job assisting a cross-cultural psychologist interested in how spatial perception in people from a non-Western culture differs from that of individuals from Western society. She has been conducting research recently with a group of people living in an isolated mountain community with no roads, no television, and little contact with outsiders. Several of them agree to participate in your research. It's exciting to have the opportunity to examine spatial perception from a cross-cultural perspective.

**Questions to Answer**

1.    How would you expect the three-dimensional perceptual abilities of these participants to compare with those of individuals from your own culture?

2.    These individuals have had no exposure to Western architecture. What influence might this have on their perceptual abilities? Compared with an individual from a city, would you expect them to be more or less susceptible to the *Müller-Lyer* illusion? What about the *Ponzo* illusion? Why?

3.    If, as young children, these individuals had participated in research employing the "visual cliff" apparatus, how would you have expected them to react?

According to Gibson's theory of direct perception, how would they react compared to children reared in Western society?

4.    Based on your research, what conclusions would you likely draw regarding the influence of culture and experience on perception?

# PART THREE:    TEST AND KNOW
# SAMPLE TEST QUESTIONS

Test how well you have learned this chapter's material by answering the sample test questions.  You may wish to mark your answers on a separate sheet of paper so you can reuse this test for exam review.  Once you have completed the exam, check your answers and then go back to your notes and the textbook to review questions you found difficult.

1.    Which of the following features is *not* shared by all sensory modalities?

   a.    a one-to-one correspondence between physical and psychological reality
   b.    the ability to translate physical stimulation into sensory signals
   c.    the ability to detect changes in stimulation
   d.    a specific threshold -- below which a person does not sense anything, despite external stimulation

2.    Some creatures obtain information about the size, location, and movement of objects through the use of _____, which involves emitting waves of sound which bounce off objects in the environment.

   a.    transduction
   b.    signal detection
   c.    difference thresholds
   d.    echolocation

3.    One type of correct response that may be given by subjects participating in a signal detection experiment is a correct negative. In this event, the subject would report

   a.    a stimulus when an actual stimulus was presented
   b.    a stimulus when no actual stimulus was presented
   c.    no stimulus when no actual stimulus was presented
   d.    no stimulus, when an actual stimulus was presented

4.    Focusing in the eye occurs in the

    a.    iris
    b.    retina
    c.    lens
    d.    aqueous humor

5.    The central region of the retina, which is sensitive to small detail and provides maximal visual acuity is the

    a.    vitreous humor
    b.    fovea
    c.    rods
    d.    optic nerve

6.    _____ or _____ occurs when the cornea and lens focus an image in front of the retina. By the time rays of light reach the retina, they have begun to cross, leading to a blurred image.

    a.    Nearsightedness; myopia
    b.    Farsightedness; myopia
    c.    Nearsightedness; hyperopia
    d.    Farsightedness; hyperopia

7.    Transduction in the eye starts with

    a.    impulses from the optic nerve passing through the optic tracts
    b.    visual information traveling to the primary visual cortex, in the occipital lobes
    c.    neurons in the lateral geniculate nucleus receiving input from the reticular formation
    d.    the focusing of images onto the retina

8.    A neurologist has just shown Samir an object, but Samir denies seeing it. Yet, when asked to describe the geometrical form of the object, Samir is able to do so with accuracy far better than one would expect simply by chance. The neurologist is likely to diagnose Samir as suffering from

    a.    amnesia.
    b.    blindsight.
    c.    hyperopia.
    d.    kinesthesia.

9.  Which of the following theories argues that all colors are derived from three color systems: a black-white system, a blue-yellow system, and a red-green system?

    a.  Place theory
    b.  Opponent-process theory
    c.  Stevens's power law
    d.  Gate-control theory

10. People recognize each other's voices, as well as the sounds of different musical instruments, from their characteristic

    a.  frequency          b.  pitch
    c.  timbre             d.  amplitude

11. The outer boundary of the middle ear is marked by the _____.

    a.  eustachian tube
    b.  cochlea
    c.  malleus
    d.  tympanic membrane

12. In terms of sensing pitch, *place theory* holds that

    a.  different areas of the basilar membrane are maximally sensitive to different frequencies
    b.  the more frequently a sound wave cycles, the more frequently the basilar membrane vibrates and hair cells fire
    c.  neurons may stagger their responses, so that the combined pattern produces a signal of a particular frequency
    d.  all of the above

13. Gustatory information travels to one of two destinations in the brain: one via the thalamus to the primary gustatory cortex, and the other to the limbic system. People with damage to the cortical first pathway, but not to the second

    a.  fail to identify substances by taste, but react with appropriate affective and behavioral responses to tastes
    b.  can identify substances by taste, but fail to show appropriate affective or behavioral response to tastes
    c.  cannot identify substances by taste and fail to react with the appropriate affective and behavioral responses to tastes
    d.  can identify substances by taste and show an immediate affective or behavioral response to tastes

14.    The approximately _____ square feet of skin covering the human body
       constitutes a complex, multilayered organ.

       a.    2                              b.    10
       c.    18                             d.    25

15.    People spend billions of dollars a year fighting pain, but pain serves an
       important function in that

       a.    it builds character
       b.    it prevents tissue damage
       c.    it indicates the presence of the disorder "painful neuropathy"
       d.    it distracts us from the worries of modern life

16.    Chronic pain patients tend to

       a.    blame their physical condition for all life's difficulties, while denying
             emotional and interpersonal problems
       b.    be anxious, needy, and dependent
       c.    have difficulty expressing anger
       d.    all of the above

17.    The two organs that transduce vestibular information are called _____, and are
       located _____.

       a.    the semicircular canals and the vestibular sacs; in the inner ear
       b.    the tendons and the muscles; in the joints
       c.    the pinna and the tympanic membrane; in the outer ear
       d.    the cochlea and the vestibular sacs; in the middle ear

18.    Which of the following is *not* a major perceptual rule by which the brain
       automatically and unconsciously organizes sensory input into meaningful
       wholes, as proposed by Gestalt psychologists?

       a.    proximity                      b.    shading
       c.    good continuation              d.    simplicity

19.    Generating meaning from sensory experience is the task of

       a.    perceptual organization
       b.    direct perception
       c.    perceptual interpretation
       d.    perceptual constancy

20.    According to current thinking, perception proceeds

  a. directly
  b. simultaneously, from the bottom-up and from the top-down
  c. from the top-down
  d. from the bottom-up

# ANSWERS

## FILL-IN EXERCISES

1. sensations; perceptions  2. absolute threshold  3. phenomenological  4. difference threshold  5. Stevens's power  6. cones; rods  7. feature detectors  8. hue, saturation, lightness  9. 15; 20,000  10. outer; pinna  11. conduction; sensorineural  12. sweet, sour, salty, bitter.  13. taste buds; papillae  14. face, fingers; back, legs  15. pain  16. kinesthesia; vestibular  17. form perception  18. interposition  19. motion detectors  20. perceptual interpretation  21. perceptual sets

## APPLICATION

1. Their experience with binocular and many monocular cues would provide information about depth. Their depth perception should, therefore, be as good as that of anyone else.
2. Lack of roads joining at angles, rectangular buildings, and so on would result in less experience with the kinds of cues that give rise to Müller-Lyer illusion. Lack of experience with lines converging in the distance (e.g., roads, railway tracks) would lead to less susceptibility to Ponzo illusion.
3. As they began to crawl, they would have been reluctant to cross to the deep side of the cliff.  According to Gibson's theory, both the understanding of depth cues and the meaning of falling off the cliff may be inborn in humans.
4. Early experience shapes the neural systems underlying sensation and perception. Some perceptual abilities are influenced by culture-specific experiences (e.g., architecture and angles); others seem uninfluenced by culture (e.g., avoidance of deep side on visual cliff)  and may even be innate.

## SAMPLE TEST QUESTIONS

|     |   |     |   |
| --- | - | --- | - |
| 1.  | a | 11. | d |
| 2.  | d | 12. | a |
| 3.  | c | 13. | a |
| 4.  | c | 14. | c |
| 5.  | b | 15. | b |
| 6.  | a | 16. | d |
| 7.  | d | 17. | a |
| 8.  | b | 18. | b |
| 9.  | b | 19. | c |
| 10. | c | 20. | b |

# Chapter 5
# LEARNING

## PART ONE:    PRE-READ AND WORK
## OUTLINE AND LEARNING OBJECTIVES

Pre-read this chapter's table of contents and end-of-chapter summary.  Then, use the outline segment-by-segment to help you work through the chapter. Jot down your own questions, comments, and notes in the space provided. Make a note of key terms and of difficult areas that you will need to review (include page numbers). Then, answer the questions in the learning objectives section that follows. Check off those you are confident that you can answer well. Re-read the material in the text for the questions about which you are less confident. Record the important points from your reading in the space below each question.

## OUTLINE

I.    CLASSICAL CONDITIONING

A. Pavlov's Model

B. Conditioned Responses

C. Stimulus Generalization and Discrimination

D. Extinction

E. Factors That Affect Classical Conditioning

F. What Do Organisms Learn in Classical Conditioning?

G. **From Mind to Brain:** The Neural Basis of Classical Conditioning

## II.    OPERANT CONDITIONING

A. Reinforcement

B. Punishment

C. Extinction

D. Operant Conditioning of Complex Behaviors

F. Similar Processes in Classical and Operant Conditioning

H. **One Step Further:** Why Are Reinforcers Reinforcing?

III.  COGNITIVE SOCIAL THEORY

A. Learning and Cognition

B. **A Global Vista:** Optimism, Pessimism, and Expectancies of Control in Cross-Cultural Perspective

C. Social Learning

IV.  SOME CONCLUDING THOUGHTS

## LEARNING OBJECTIVES

Upon completion of Chapter 5, you should be able to answer the following questions.

1. What are the three assumptions shared by theories of learning?

2. What are the basic principles underlying Pavlov's model of conditioning?

3. What are the differences between an unconditioned stimulus (UCS) and a conditioned stimulus (CS), and between an unconditioned response (UCR) and a conditioned response (CR)?

4.    How did John Watson produce a conditioned emotional response in little Albert?

5.    How can the functioning of the immune system be affected by classical conditioning?

6.    How does stimulus generalization differ from stimulus discrimination?

7.    What is involved in the processes of extinction and spontaneous recovery?

8.    What are the differences between forward, simultaneous, and backward conditioning?

9.    Discuss the notion that animals may be biologically prepared to learn some associations more easily than others.

10.    What is the phenomenon of paradoxical conditioning?

11.    How does reinforcement differ from punishment? Provide illustrations of positive and negative reinforcement, as well as positive and negative punishment.

12.    What are five common drawbacks associated with the use of punishment?

13.    How does partial reinforcement differ from continuous reinforcement? Describe four types of partial reinforcement schedules and their effects on responding.

14. Provide several everyday examples of discriminative stimuli signaling the occurrence of particular contingencies of reinforcement.

15. Explain what is meant by the term "behavioral economics."

16. How can shaping and chaining be used to teach complex behaviors?

17. How does operant learning theory explain superstitious behavior?

18. How does drive reduction account for the reinforcing value of certain stimuli?

19. How do secondary reinforcers acquire their reinforcing properties?

20. What are the roles of the behavioral approach system (BAS) and the behavioral inhibition system (BIS) in the learning of operant behavior?

21. How does the phenomenon of latent learning provide evidence for the role of cognition in learning?

22. What is meant by the term locus of control? How do people with an internal locus of control differ from those with an external locus of control?

23. In what ways do individuals with a pessimistic explanatory style interpret negative events in a depressive manner?

24.    What is involved in the phenomenon of social learning and how is this important in the cognitive social theory of learning?

25.    How can a person learn the consequences of behavior through the process of vicarious conditioning?

## PART TWO:    REVIEW AND LEARN
## KEY TERMS, FILL-IN EXERCISES, APPLICATION AND USING WHAT YOU HAVE LEARNED

Before doing the exercises below, review the information you learned in this chapter. Reread the work you did in part one of this study guide chapter, plus the interim summaries and end-of-chapter summary in your textbook. Review any problem areas. Once you feel comfortable with the material, do the following exercises without referring to your notes or textbook. If you have difficulty with a term or question, mark it and come back to it. When you have finished an exercise, go back to your notes and the textbook to find the answers to the questions that gave you difficulty. Finally, check your answers (key terms against the textbook and the rest against the answer key).

## KEY TERMS

Laws of association _____

_____

Classical conditioning     _____

_____

Reflex _____

_____

Stimulus     _____

_____

Conditioning_____

_____

Unconditioned stimulus (UCS)    _____

_____

Unconditioned response (UCR)    _____

_____

Conditioned response (CR)    _____

_____

Conditioned stimulus (CS)_____

_____

Conditioned taste aversion_____

_____

Conditioned emotional response    _____

_____

Phobias    _____

_____

Stimulus generalization    _____

_____

Galvanic skin response (GSR)    _____

_____

Stimulus discrimination    _____

_____

Acquisition _____

_____

Conditioning trial _____

_____

Extinction _____

_____

Spontaneous recovery _____

_____

Interstimulus interval _____

_____

Forward conditioning _____

_____

Simultaneous conditioning_____

_____

Backward conditioning _____

_____

Blocking _____

_____

Latent inhibition _____

_____

Prepared learning _____

_____

Paradoxical conditioning _____

_____

Law of effect _____

_____

Operant conditioning _____

_____

Operants _____

_____

Reinforcement _____

_____

Punishment _____

_____

Reinforcer _____

_____

Positive reinforcement _____

_____

Positive reinforcer _____

_____

Negative reinforcement _____

_____

Negative reinforcer _____

_____

Escape learning _____

_____

Avoidance learning _____

_____

Positive punishment _____

_____

Negative punishment _____

_____

Continuous reinforcement schedule _____

_____

Partial or intermittent schedule _____

_____

Fixed ratio (FR) schedule _____

_____

Variable ratio (VR) schedule _____

_____

Fixed interval (FI) schedule _____

_____

Variable interval (VI) schedule _____

_____

Discriminative stimulus _____

_____

Shaping _____

_____

Chaining _____

_____

Biofeedback _____

_____

Drive-reduction theory _____

_____

Primary reinforcers _____

_____

Secondary reinforcers _____

_____

Behavioral approach system (BAS) _____

_____

Behavioral inhibition system (BIS) _____

_____

Cognitive-social theory _____

_____

Cognitive maps _____

_____

Latent learning _____

_____

Outcome expectancy _____

_____

Locus of control of reinforcement _____

_____

Internal locus of control _____

_____

External locus of control _____

_____

Learned helplessness _____

_____

Explanatory style _____

_____

Social learning _____

_____

Observational learning _____

_____

Modeling _____

_____

Vicarious conditioning _____

_____

Tutelage _____

_____

## FILL-IN EXERCISES

Fill in the word or words that best fit in the spaces below.

1.  Classical conditioning involves associating a neutral stimulus with the _____ stimulus. Following several trials, the neutral stimulus will come to elicit the response, and is now referred to as the _____ stimulus.

2.  The fear response that little Albert displayed to the white rat in Watson and Rayner's study is an example of a _____ _____ response.

3.  Little Albert's fear of other stimuli that shared certain characteristics with the rat (i.e., furry or hairy objects) is a good example of the phenomenon of _____ _____.

4.  Galvanic skin response (GSR) is an electrical measure of the amount of sweat on the skin and can be used to assess _____.

5.  Each pairing of the CS and UCS is know as a conditioning _____.

6.  Presentation of the CS without the UCS will lead to _____ of the CR.

7.  The duration of time between presentation of the CS and UCS is referred to as the _____ _____.

8.  _____ conditioning involves presenting the CS after the UCS has occurred.

9.  The failure of a stimulus to elicit a conditioned response when it is combined with another stimulus that is already effective in eliciting the response is called _____.

10. Fear of snakes and spiders in humans may involve the learning of associations that are biologically _____.

11. Operants are behaviors that are _____ by the organism rather than _____ by the environment.

12. Negative reinforcement _____ the probability that a response will occur.

13. The unannounced, unexpected arrival of the health inspector at the door of the neighborhood restaurant is an example of a _____ _____ schedule of reinforcement.

14.    Psychologists use _____ to help patients to gain control over autonomic responses such as heart rate, body temperature, and blood pressure by feeding them information about these responses.

15.    A _____ is a state that impels the organism to act.

16.    _____ _____ refers to the expectancy that one cannot escape aversive events, which leads to motivational and learning deficits.

## APPLICATION

### Situation

After his class attended a special kids' performance of the symphony, 8-year-old Billy had been begging his parents to buy him a violin. Finally, they gave in and got him one. The only problem is that he doesn't practice. His teacher says he should practice for half an hour each day, but Billy never does more than 5 minutes. His mom keeps nagging him to practice, but it doesn't work. He practices for 5 minutes, and then he's off to his friend's house. His mom is getting frustrated and is considering canceling his lessons. Having just studied learning in her psychology course, she decides to try applying operant learning principles to change Billy's behavior. She buys a Nintendo, to use to reward Billy for practicing for half an hour each day. She realizes, however, that half an hour of practice will initially seem like an eternity to him, and he'll probably give up after only 10 minutes. So, she gets her kitchen timer and tells Billy: "I want you to practice your violin until the bell on the timer rings. When it rings, come and get me and we'll play Nintendo together." The first day, she sets the timer for 5 minutes. The next day, she sets it for 10 minutes. The next day she sets it for 15 minutes, and so on. By the end of the week, Billy is practicing for half an hour.

### Questions to Answer

1.    In the above situation, playing Nintendo with mom serves as what?

2.    Rewarding Billy for practicing his violin for a progressively longer time is an example of what?

3.    The bell on the timer serves as what kind of stimulus?

After a couple of weeks, Billy's mom is pleased that he is practicing for half an hour a day, but is finding that she hasn't got the time to play Nintendo with him every day. Yet, when she told him she hasn't got time to play Nintendo any more, Billy's practicing time dropped back to 5 minutes.

4.      Billy's drop in practice time after his mom stopped playing Nintendo with him is an example of what principle of learning?

5.      In terms of operant learning theory, how could Billy's mom cut back on playing Nintendo, but still keep Billy regularly practicing for half an hour?

## USING WHAT YOU HAVE LEARNED

One of the most difficult problems parents face is when their children display temper tantrums. Kids will scream, roll around on the floor, bang their hands and heads on the floor, hold their breath, and so on until they get what they want. Parents are often embarrassed or concerned that their child might hurt himself or herself. So they often "give in" and let the child have what he or she wanted in order to end the tantrum.

In terms of reinforcement, what do you suppose happens when parents give in to the tantrum? How will this likely affect the probability of future tantrums?

If giving in stops the tantrum (an aversive stimulus), what are parents likely to do the next time the child throws a tantrum? Why?

Often, children learn that there are certain places where parents will give in quickly, such as on the bus or in a quiet place like a library. Kids are all the more likely to throw a tantrum in these places. What do these situations signal to the child? What would be the behavioral term to apply to these situations?

What would you advise parents to do to stop the tantrums, based on your understanding of the principles of learning?

## PART THREE:   TEST AND KNOW
## SAMPLE TEST QUESTIONS

Test how well you have learned this chapter's material by answering the sample test questions.  You may wish to mark your answers on a separate sheet of paper so you can reuse this test for exam review.  Once you have completed the exam, check your answers and then go back to your notes and the textbook to review questions you found difficult.

1.      Praise is a good example of a(n)

    a.      conditioned stimulus          b.      unconditioned stimulus
    c.      secondary reinforcer          d.      vicarious reinforcer

2.    Slot machines are popular in casinos because all you have to do to play is pull the lever. Every so often, after an unpredictable number of pulls, somebody will "hit the jackpot." What schedule of reinforcement is likely in effect here?

    a.    fixed interval
    b.    fixed ratio
    c.    variable interval
    d.    variable ratio

3.    The fact that people will put money into slot machines and pull the level over and over, especially after seeing someone else hit the jackpot, even though they may have never won anything themselves can be explained in terms of

    a.    vicarious learning
    b.    avoidance learning
    c.    classical conditioning
    d.    operant conditioning

4.    Tolman suggested that rats may form _____ , or mental representations of a maze, even without any reinforcement.

    a.    cognitive maps
    b.    generalized expectancies
    c.    outcome expectancies
    d.    all of the above

5.    Many people display severe negative emotional reactions to hypodermic needles, through exposure to injections in childhood. These reactions can be explained in terms of:

    a.    instrumental conditioning
    b.    classical conditioning
    c.    blocking
    d.    preparedness to learn

6.    Suppose Watson and Raynor had exposed little Albert repeatedly (i.e., on the second, third, and all subsequent trials) to the white rat but without the noise.

    a.    Albert's fear response would have become even stronger.
    b.    Albert's fear response would have generalized to whatever white, furry objects were present in the environment.
    c.    Albert's fear response would have extinguished.
    d.    Albert's fear response would have spontaneously recovered.

7.  In classical conditioning, the least effective form of temporal relationship between the CS and UCS involves

    a.  forward conditioning
    b.  backward conditioning
    c.  simultaneous conditioning
    d.  paradoxical conditioning

8.  The sight of drug paraphernalia can activate physiological reactions that reduce the effect of the heroin an addict is about to take. This likely involves

    a.  stimulus substitution
    b.  escape learning
    c.  vicarious conditioning
    d.  paradoxical conditioning

9.  Learning to drive a car with a manual transmission involves acquiring a variety of behaviors, such as shifting the gears, using the clutch, using the accelerator, and so on. Putting these together to drive the car smoothly involves

    a.  chaining          b.  escape learning
    c.  shaping           d.  simultaneous conditioning

10. Keeping your driving speed below the speed limit so you don't get caught in a radar trap is an example of

    a.  avoidance learning
    b.  escape learning
    c.  shaping
    d.  positive punishment

11. Removing a child's TV privileges is an example of

    a.  negative reinforcement
    b.  negative punishment
    c.  positive punishment
    d.  secondary reinforcement

12. Punishment tends to be most effective

    a.  when it is severe
    b.  when it occurs some time after the behavior
    c.  when it is accompanied by reasoning
    d.  punishment is *never* effective

13.    The students in Mr. Bebby's grade 8 class have learned not to fool around when he's mad, because he's likely to give the whole class detention. The easiest way to tell when he's mad is that you can see a vein on the side of his forehead begin throbbing. When that vein starts throbbing, the students immediately settle down. Mr. Bebby's throbbing vein is a

    a.    secondary reinforcer
    b.    conditioned stimulus
    c.    conditioned response
    d.    discriminative stimulus

14.    In the above example, settling down when Mr. Bebby's vein starts throbbing is an example of

    a.    superstitious behavior
    b.    a conditioned response
    c.    avoidance learning
    d.    latent learning

15.    Gray argues that anatomically distinct pathways in the nervous system control different forms of learning and are associated with different emotional states. The system involved in negative reinforcement and punishment is

    a.    the behavioral approach system
    b.    the behavioral inhibition system
    c.    the fight-flight system
    d.    the latent inhibition system

16.    Learning that has occurred, but is not currently manifest in behavior, was described by Tolman as

    a.    latent learning
    b.    discriminative learning
    c.    vicarious learning
    d.    escape learning

17.    Everything has been going wrong for Ted. No matter what he tries, it doesn't seem to make any difference. So, he's just given up trying. Ted's behavior is an example of

    a.    avoidance learning
    b.    backward conditioning
    c.    stimulus generalization
    d.    learned helplessness

18. All of the following *except* one are ways in which individuals with a pessimistic explanatory style see the causes of negative events. Which does not apply?

    a. internal
    b. stable
    c. global
    d. temporary

19. Fishing involves behavior that is difficult to extinguish. People who like fishing will spend hours "on the lake" without catching anything, before finally giving up in frustration. This is because fishing likely involves

    a. a conditioned emotional response
    b. backward conditioning
    c. intermittent reinforcement
    d. tutelage

20. After seeing a child get bitten by a dog, little Mario displays an intense fear reaction when he sees a puppy at the pet store. His response can be explained with reference to

    a. classical conditioning
    b. vicarious conditioning
    c. instrumental conditioning
    d. backward conditioning

# ANSWERS

## FILL-IN EXERCISES

1. unconditioned; conditioned  2. conditioned emotional  3. stimulus generalization
4. arousal (or anxiety)  5. trial  6. extinction  7. interstimulus interval  8. backward
9. blocking  10. prepared  11. emitted; elicited  12. increases  13. variable interval
14. biofeedback  15. drive  16. learned helplessness

## APPLICATION

1. A positive reinforcer  2. Shaping  3. A discriminative stimulus  4. Extinction
5. Partial reinforcement (variable ratio schedule)

## SAMPLE TEST QUESTIONS

| | | | |
|---|---|---|---|
| 1. | c | 11. | b |
| 2. | d | 12. | c |
| 3. | a | 13. | d |
| 4. | a | 14. | c |
| 5. | b | 15. | b |
| 6. | c | 16. | a |
| 7. | b | 17. | d |
| 8. | d | 18. | d |
| 9. | a | 19. | c |
| 10. | a | 20. | b |

# Chapter 6
# MEMORY

## PART ONE:  PRE-READ AND WORK
## OUTLINE AND LEARNING OBJECTIVES

Pre-read this chapter's table of contents and end-of-chapter summary.  Then, use the outline segment-by-segment to help you work through the chapter. Jot down your own questions, comments, and notes in the space provided. Make a note of difficult areas that you will need to review (include page numbers). Then, answer the questions in the learning objectives section that follows. Check off those you are confident that you can answer well. Re-read the material in the text for the questions about which you are less confident. Record the important points from your reading in the space below each question.

## OUTLINE

I.  MEMORY AND INFORMATION PROCESSING

    A. Mental Representations

    B. Information Processing: An Evolving Model

II.  WORKING MEMORY

    A. Processing Information in Working Memory: The Central Executive

    B. Visual and Verbal Storage

    C. **One Step Further:** The Neuropsychology of Working Memory

D. The Relation Between Working Memory and Long-Term Memory

## III. VARIETIES OF LONG-TERM MEMORY

A. Declarative and Procedural Memory

B. Explicit and Implicit Memory

C. **From Mind to Brain:** The Neuropsychology of Long-Term Memory

D. Everyday Memory

## IV. ENCODING AND ORGANIZATION OF LONG-TERM MEMORY

A. Encoding

B. Mnemonic Devices

C. Networks of Association

D. Schemas

E. **A Global Vista:** Cross-Cultural Variation in Memory – Better, Worse, or Just Different?

## V. REMEMBERING, MISREMEMBERING, AND FORGETTING

A. How Long is Long-Term Memory?

B. How Accurate is Long-Term Memory?

C. Why do People Forget?

D. **Commentary:** Repressed Memories of Sexual Abuse

## VI. SOME CONCLUDING THOUGHTS

## LEARNING OBJECTIVES

Upon completion of Chapter 6, you should be able to answer the following questions.

1.    In what ways do sensory representations differ from verbal representations?

2.    How does iconic storage differ from echoic storage?

3.    What are the major differences between long-term and short-term memory?

4.    How does serial position affect free recall?

5.    What are four major ways in which thinking about memory has evolved over the past decade?

6.    Discuss the storage and processing functions of working memory.

7.    What evidence does neurological research provide for the notion of working memory?

8.    How are working memory and long-term memory related?

9.    What are the differences between declarative and procedural memory?

10.    How does explicit memory differ from implicit memory?

11. What evidence does neurological research provide for the distinction between explicit and implicit memory?

12. What has recent research revealed about everyday memory?

13. How is the accessibility of information in long-term memory influenced by the following: level of processing; encoding specificity; spacing; and representational modes?

14. What are three common forms of mnemonic devices?

15. Explain how pieces of information stored in memory form networks of association.

16. In what ways is hierarchical organization of information analogous to a filing system?

17. How are both encoding and retrieval of information affected by schemas?

18. How can the organization of information in memory be influenced by culture?

19. Why are some researchers concerned about the accuracy of eyewitness testimony in the courtroom?

20. What are the differences between the following three explanations of forgetting: decay, interference, and motivated forgetting?

21.    Why is it difficult to scientifically address the issue of false memories of childhood trauma?

## PART TWO:    REVIEW AND LEARN
## KEY TERMS, FILL-IN EXERCISES, APPLICATION AND USING WHAT YOU HAVE LEARNED

Before doing the exercises below, review the information you learned in this chapter. Reread the work you did in part one of this study guide chapter, plus the interim summaries and end-of-chapter summary in your textbook.  Review any problem areas. Once you feel comfortable with the material, do the following exercises without referring to your notes or textbook.  If you have difficulty with a term or question, mark it and come back to it.  When you have finished an exercise, go back to your notes and the textbook to find the answers to the questions that gave you difficulty.  Finally, check your answers (key terms against the textbook and the rest against the answer key).

## KEY TERMS

Upon completion of Chapter 6, you should be able to define the following terms.

Sensory representations    _____

_____

Verbal representations    _____

_____

Sensory registers    _____

_____

Iconic storage    _____

_____

Echoic storage    _____

_____

Short-term memory (STM) _____

_____

Maintenance rehearsal _____

_____

Elaborative rehearsal _____

_____

Long-term memory _____

_____

Retrieval _____

_____

Memory systems _____

_____

Working memory _____

_____

Chunking _____

_____

Declarative memory _____

_____

Semantic memory _____

_____

Episodic memory _____

_____

Procedural memory _____

_____

Explicit memory _____

_____

Recall _____

_____

Recognition _____

_____

Implicit memory _____

_____

Everyday memory _____

_____

Prospective memory _____

_____

Encoding _____

_____

Level of processing _____

_____

Retrieval cues _____

_____

Spacing _____

_____

Mnemonic devices _____

_____

Networks of association  _____

_____

Spreading activation theory    _____

_____

Hierarchical organization  _____

_____

Schemas    _____

_____

Flashbulb memories    _____

_____

Decay theory_____

_____

Proactive interference    _____

_____

Retroactive interference    _____

_____

Motivated forgetting    _____

_____

## FILL-IN EXERCISES

Fill in the word or words that best fit in the spaces below.

1. People maintain a mental image (icon) of what they have seen that lasts for approximately _____ to _____ seconds. Presenting another image or even a flash of light directly after the first image disappears will _____ the original icon.

2. Some researchers have suggested that humans have two types of _____ memory systems, one for nonspeech sounds and the other for speech.

3. Short-term memory holds information in consciousness for approximately _____ to _____ seconds, unless the person makes a deliberate attempt to retain it longer by repeating it over and over.

4. On the average, people can hold about _____ pieces of information in STM, with the normal range from _____ to _____ items.

5. The tendency for subjects to remember words at the beginning of a list better than words that appear later is known as the _____ effect.

6. Information remains in _____ memory only so long as the person is consciously processing, examining, or manipulating it.

7. According to one prominent model, working memory consists of three memory systems: a _____ memory store, a _____ memory store, and a _____ _____ that controls and manipulates the information that these two short-term stores hold in mind.

8. Memory for facts and events, much of which can be consciously stated, is referred to as _____ memory.

9. Memory that is expressed in behavior but does not require conscious recollection is referred to as _____ memory.

10. Neurological research indicates that the neural structure known as the _____ is crucial to the consolidation of explicit memories.

11. _____ memory has at least two components: remembering *to* remember (or intent) and remembering *what* to remember (or content).

12.    According to the _____ _____ principle, the contexts in which people encode and retrieve information can affect the ease of retrieval.

13.    _____ devices are strategies that people use as memory aids.

14.    Networks of association involve complex interconnections among _____.

15.    Information in LTM tends to be filed _____.

## USING WHAT YOU HAVE LEARNED

A group of university students listened to a news report describing how an airline pilot courageously landed a plane safely after its landing gear had failed.

After hearing this story, most of the students described the aircraft as a jet, although there was no mention in the story of what type of aircraft it was. In addition, several of them added details that were not in the news report, such as describing the pilot as male, or adding the observation that it had been raining at the time of the landing. What type of memory do these phenomena involve? What is likely responsible for the addition of new information about the type of aircraft, the sex of the pilot, and the weather conditions? Have you ever noticed similar errors in your own recall of specific details of events? Could there be any advantage to such aspects of memory?

## APPLICATION

### Situation

A friend of yours, knowing that you are studying psychology and that you have just finished learning about memory, asks for your advice in how to prepare for an upcoming exam. In terms of what you have covered in this chapter, how would you answer her questions?

1. "When I get into the exam I always just go blank. Are there any 'memory tricks' that will help me remember the important concepts I have to remember?"

2. "I find it best to stay up all night and cram the night before. The only problem is that some of this material will also be on the final next month. Is there a better way to study so that I'll remember more for the final?"

3. "Is it best just to read my notes over and over, or is there some other thing I could be doing?"

4. "Someone told me that it's better to study the material in a different order every time I go over it. You know, tomorrow begin with the material I studied in the middle tonight and end with the beginning material. Next night, begin with the end material. Is there any truth to that? Why would that help?"

5. "Sometimes I find that studying for Italian actually makes it harder to remember the material I previously studied for my French exam. Am I just fooling myself, or could this really happen?"

## PART THREE:    TEST AND KNOW
## SAMPLE TEST QUESTIONS

Test how well you have learned this chapter's material by answering the sample test questions. You may wish to mark your answers on a separate sheet of paper so you can reuse this test for exam review. Once you have completed the exam, check your answers and then go back to your notes and the textbook to review questions you found difficult.

1.    Repeating information over and over again to prevent it from fading is a procedure known as

    a.    rehearsal
    b.    chunking
    c.    echoic storage
    d.    SQ3R method

2.    When a list of items is presented to subjects, they tend to remember items at the end of the list more easily than those in the middle, because of

    a.    rehearsal
    b.    the recency effect
    c.    the priming process
    d.    schematic processing

3.    Baddeley and Hitch had subjects perform two tasks simultaneously: one involved recalling a series of digits and the other involved some kind of thinking, such as reasoning or comprehending the meaning of sentences. Their results suggested that

    a.    storage capacity and processing capacity are two separate aspects of working memory
    b.    storage capacity and processing capacity are ultimately the same thing; they are highly interdependent
    c.    short-term memory is too limited to involve working on two tasks simultaneously
    d.    while storage capacity in STM is unlimited, processing capacity is limited to a small number of tasks

4.    Working memory appears to be "directed" by the _____, a region of the brain long known to be involved in most high-level cognitive functions.

    a.    hippocampus
    b.    hypothalamus
    c.    prefrontal cortex
    d.    occipital cortex

5.    In a memory experiment involving recall of a series of digits, one subject reported treating the digits like phone numbers, breaking the series down into a 3-digit "area code," a 7-digit "phone number," and a 4-digit "extension." Using this procedure, the subject was able to hold 14 digits in STM. This procedure is an example of

    a.    the method of loci
    b.    semantic processing
    c.    spacing of rehearsal
    d.    chunking

6.    Declarative memory can involve either _____ or _____ memory.

    a.    semantic; phonemic
    b.    semantic; structural
    c.    explicit; implicit
    d.    semantic; episodic

7.    Multiple choice tests, such as this, likely involve which type of retrieval from LTM?

    a.    recognition
    b.    recall
    c.    primary
    d.    secondary

8.    In a classical conditioning procedure in which a tone is paired with electric shock, patients with an intact hippocampus but a damaged amygdala

    a.    have no conscious idea that the tone is associated with shock, but show a conditioned fear response to it nonetheless
    b.    consciously know that the tone is associated with shock, and show a conditioned fear response to it
    c.    consciously know that the tone is associated with shock, but show no conditioned fear response to it
    d.    have no conscious idea that the tone is associated with shock, nor show a conditioned fear response to it

9.    Melanie ties a string around her finger in the morning, so she won't forget to pick up a loaf of bread on her way home from work. What aspect of memory is involved in this situation?

   a.   working memory           b.   procedural memory
   c.   implicit memory          d.   prospective memory

10.   Many students report that it is much easier for them to recall information when they write an in-class test in the same room as they take a the course than when they write the final examination in an examination hall or the gym. A possible reason for this difference is

   a.   interference             b.   retrieval cues
   c.   motivated forgetting     d.   memory decay

11.   Driving to school, Maria was mentally rehearsing for her psychology exam. To help remember the important topics for the exam, she created a ridiculous mental image of the topics being scattered around her bedroom -- on the bed, under the pillow, under the bed, on her desk, and so on. As she drove along, she suddenly realized that she had driven 3 miles without even paying attention to her driving. Yet she had not run any red lights, and she had used her clutch properly and not stalled while shifting gears. This unconscious, automatic behavior could be described as involving

   a.   declarative memory
   b.   implicit memory
   c.   episodic memory
   d.   short-term memory

12.   Maria's method of trying to remember the important topics for her exam, in the above question, involves using

   a.   the method of loci
   b.   the SQ3R method
   c.   the peg method
   d.   none of the above

13.   "First I have to get money from the bank, then I have to pick up the clothes at the cleaners, then I have to get the kids at school, then get milk at the corner store. How will I remember? Let's see, 'One is a bun,' OK, money in the bun; 'two is a shoe,' clothes go with shoes; 'three is a tree,' kids climb in trees; 'four is a door,' the milk is by the door." This is a good example of

   a.   the method of loci        b.   the peg method
   c.   the SQ3R method           d.   constructive memory

14.    Pieces of information along a network of associations are called _____.

a.    nodes
b.    loci
c.    files
d.    pegs

15.    Schemas play an important role in helping to process new information and enter it into memory. Schemas can also result in processing and retrieval errors. Which of the following errors could be attributable to schemas?

a.    leading people to misclassify information
b.    causing people to believe they have seen information that really was not present
c.    causing people to fail to notice information that might be important
d.    all of the above

16.    Cross-cultural research on memory indicates that

a.    people tend to remember information that matters to them and what really matters is the same across cultures
b.    cross-cultural variations in performance on memory tasks are the result of differences between cultures in memory capacity
c.    differences within a culture are so great as to obscure any cross-cultural differences
d.    cross-cultural differences seem to result from differences in how people schematically organize information

17.    Manal remembers sitting with her brother in the living room of her parents' home, wearing her pajamas, when she saw the space shuttle Challenger disaster on TV. Such vivid memories of exciting or highly consequential events are referred to as

a.    flashbulb memories
b.    emotional memories
c.    retrospective memories
d.    implicit memories

18.    Research on forgetting shows that

a.    forgetting follows a typical pattern with a gradual initial loss of information, with the rate of loss increasing with time
b.    the pace at which information is forgotten is quite different when the time period is hours than when the time period is years
c.    the decline of memory is logarithmically related to the length of time between learning and retrieval
d.    all of the above

19.    Dave's friend Andrea has a different computer from Dave, with a different word processing program on it. Dave found it very hard to use Andrea's computer. "It just doesn't make sense," he said. "I didn't have this much trouble learning my program. But now I can't get the commands straight at all!" This problem where previously stored memories interfere with the retrieval of new information is called

    a.    retroactive interference
    b.    motivated forgetting
    c.    proactive interference
    d.    state-dependent learning

20.    Dave tried really hard to learn the second program. He got so confused after learning the second program that he could no longer remember the commands for the first program. His problem now is due to

    a.    retroactive interference
    b.    repression
    c.    proactive interference
    d.    state-dependent learning

# ANSWERS

## FILL-IN EXERCISES

1. ½ , two; erase   2. echoic   3. 20, 30   4. seven; five, nine   5. primacy   6. working
7. visual; verbal; central executive 8. declarative 9. implicit   10. hippocampus
11. prospective   12. encoding specificity   13. mnemonic   14. nodes   15. hierarchically

## APPLICATION

1. Yes. Use mnemonic devices such as *loci* method and *peg* method.
2. Yes. Space rehearsal over a period of time.
3. Don't just read notes over and over. Use encoding strategies. Form associative links to previously stored information. Elaborate and reflect upon the information (depth of processing). Use a variety of representational modes and mnemonic devices (especially try SQ3R method).
4. Yes. Serial position effects
5. Yes. The problem is retroactive interference.

## SAMPLE TEST QUESTIONS

| 1. | a | 11. | b |
|---|---|---|---|
| 2. | b | 12. | a |
| 3. | a | 13. | b |
| 4. | c | 14. | a |
| 5. | d | 15. | d |
| 6. | d | 16. | d |
| 7. | a | 17. | a |
| 8. | c | 18. | c |
| 9. | d | 19. | c |
| 10. | b | 20. | a |

# Chapter 7
# THOUGHT AND LANGUAGE

## PART ONE:    PRE-READ AND WORK
## OUTLINE AND LEARNING OBJECTIVES

Pre-read this chapter's table of contents and end-of-chapter summary. Then, use the outline segment-by-segment to help you work through the chapter. Jot down your own questions, comments, and notes in the space provided. Make a note of difficult areas that you will need to review (include page numbers). Then, answer the questions in the learning objectives section that follows. Check off those you are confident that you can answer well. Re-read the material in the text for the questions about which you are less confident. Record the important points from your reading in the space below each question.

## OUTLINE

I.    UNITS OF THOUGHT

   A. Manipulating Mental Representations

   B. Concepts and Categories

   C. **A Global Vista:** Culture and Categorization

II.   REASONING, PROBLEM SOLVING, AND DECISION MAKING

   A. Reasoning

   B. Problem Solving

C. Decision Making

## III.   IMPLICIT AND EVERYDAY THINKING

A. How Rational are We?

B. Implicit Cognition

C. Emotion, Motivation, and Decision Making

D. Connectionism

E. **From Mind to Brain:** The Neuropsychology of Thinking

## IV.   LANGUAGE

A. Language and Thought

B. Transforming Sounds and Symbols into Meaning

## LEARNING OBJECTIVES

Upon completion of Chapter 7, you should be able to answer the following questions.

1.  How does thinking employ mental images and mental models?

2.  What are the differences between the prototype-matching and defining-features views of categorization?

3.  How do basic level, subordinate, and superordinate level categories differ?

4.  How are basic-level categories influenced by culture?

5.  How does inductive reasoning differ from deductive reasoning?

6.  How can analogical reasoning be used to help understand a novel situation?

7.  What is the difference between a well-defined and an ill-defined problem?

8.  What are the four steps involved in problem solving?

9.  Compare the advantages and disadvantages of three types of problem-solving strategies – algorithms, hypothesis testing, and mental simulation.

10. In what ways do functional fixedness and the confirmation bias interfere with rational problem solving?

11. How can the value and likelihood of options be combined in the process of decision making?

12. Describe the procedures involved in solving problems with numbers.

13. In what ways can heuristics lead to irrational judgments?

14. What is meant by the expression "bounded rationality?"

15. Explain how both learning and problem-solving can occur implicitly – that is, outside of awareness.

16. How are motives and emotions related to the way people assess risks?

17. What are the two propositions that underlie parallel distributed processing (PDP) models?

18. Explain the process of parallel constraint satisfaction.

19. Describe the consequences of damage to the dorsolateral and the ventromedial prefrontal cortex.

20. What is the Whorfian hypothesis of linguistic relativity?

21. How do morphemes differ from phonemes?

22.    How do listeners employ information about both syntax and semantics to understand the meaning of sentences?

23.    Explain what is meant by the expression "multiple levels of discourse."

24    Describe how communication is influenced by shared rules of conversation, as well as by nonverbal communication.

25.    How do behaviorists explain language acquisition? What challenges to this approach have been posed by the nativist position?

26.    Explain how the connectionist model provides an interactions view of language acquisition.

27.    What evidence is there to support the notion of a critical period for language acquisition?

28.    What are the differences between babbling and telegraphic speech?

29.    How is children's language acquisition influenced by caregiver input and feedback?

30.    How has research with chimps questioned the notion that language is unique to humans?

## PART TWO: REVIEW AND LEARN
## KEY TERMS, FILL-IN EXERCISES, APPLICATION AND USING WHAT YOU HAVE LEARNED

Before doing the exercises below, review the information you learned in this chapter. Reread the work you did in part one of this study guide chapter, plus the interim summaries and end-of-chapter summary in your textbook. Review any problem areas. Once you feel comfortable with the material, do the following exercises without referring to your notes or textbook. If you have difficulty with a term or question, mark it and come back to it. When you have finished an exercise, go back to your notes and the textbook to find the answers to the questions that gave you difficulty. Finally, check your answers (key terms against the textbook and the rest against the answer key).

## KEY TERMS

Upon completion of Chapter 7, you should be able to define the following terms.

Mental images _____

_____

Mental models _____

_____

Concepts _____

_____

Categorization _____

_____

Prototypes _____

_____

Defining features _____

_____

Basic level    _____

_____

Reasoning    _____

_____

Inductive reasoning_____

_____

Deductive reasoning    _____

_____

Analogical reasoning    _____

_____

Syllogism    _____

_____

Problem solving    _____

_____

Problem-solving strategies    _____

_____

Mental simulation    _____

_____

Operators    _____

_____

Confirmation bias    _____

_____

Functional fixedness    _____

_____

Decision making    _____

_____

Weighted utility value    _____

_____

Expected utility    _____

_____

Algorithm    _____

_____

Explicit cognition    _____

_____

Heuristic    _____

_____

Representativeness heuristic    _____

_____

Availability heuristic    _____

_____

Bounded rationality_____

_____

Implicit cognition    _____

_____

Connectionist (or parallel distributed processing) models _____

_____

Constraint satisfaction   _____

_____

Phoneme   _____

_____

Morpheme   _____

_____

Phrases   _____

_____

Sentences   _____

_____

Pragmatics   _____

_____

Discourse   _____

_____

Nonverbal communication   _____

_____

Universal grammar _____

_____

Language Acquisition Device (LAD)   _____

_____

Critical period hypothesis _____

_____

Babbling _____

_____

Telegraphic speech _____

_____

## FILL-IN EXERCISES

Fill in the word or words that best fit in the spaces below.

1.  _____ means manipulating mental representations for a purpose.

2.  _____ _____ are representations that describe, explain, or predict the way things work.

3.  The level that people naturally tend to use in categorizing objects is known as the _____ level. One level more abstract than this is the _____ level.

4.  _____ refers to the process by which people generate and evaluate logical arguments and beliefs.

5.  Reasoning from specific observations to generate propositions that are probably true is referred to as _____ _____.

6.  The process by which people understand a novel situation in terms of a familiar one is referred to as _____ _____.

7.  In a well-defined problem, the _____ state, _____ state, and the _____ are easily determined.

8.  According to information-processing models, when people make decisions, they consider the _____ as well as the _____ of the outcomes of different options.

9.  The _____ heuristic assumes that events or occurrences that can be recalled easily must be common and are therefore likely to happen.

10. "Aha" experiences, when people set aside a seemingly insoluble problem only to find hours or days later that the answer suddenly comes to them, are examples of _____ problem solving.

11. Damage to the _____ prefrontal cortex can result in difficulty connecting feelings with thought.

12. The Whorfian hypothesis of linguistic relativity holds that _____ shapes _____.

13. The grammar of nonverbal communication tends to be largely unconscious and encoded as _____ knowledge.

14. When parents provide feedback concerning their children's language, they focus on _____ rather than _____.

15. Short sentences in which children leave out all but the essential words are called _____ speech.

16. A _____ _____ refers to a point in development when the brain is maximally sensitive to language acquisition.


## APPLICATION

For each of the following situations, identify the aspect of reasoning or problem solving that is illustrated.

1. Fred has taken his lucky rabbit's foot to the last three Dodgers' games, and they've won all three. He concludes that it's because of his rabbit's foot and vows to bring it to every game from now on. He remembers bringing it to the two other games he attended, and they won both times. He overlooks the fact that they've won almost every game at home this season, even though he's only been to five. What type of reasoning led Dave to his conclusion about the rabbit's foot? What type of bias is leading to Dave's erroneous conclusion?

2. When Nancy came over to Dave's for dinner, she was surprised that he was such a good cook. "Men can't cook," reasoned Nancy. "Dave is a man; therefore, Dave can't cook." What type of reasoning led Nancy to this conclusion?

3. Jane just can't forget the news report she saw on the big plane crash at the airport in her city. Ever since then, she won't fly anywhere. "Too much chance of a crash," Jane reasons. "Driving's much safer!" What led to this error in Jane's reasoning?

4.    In screening new candidates for executive positions, Acme Tire company presents them with an Acme tire and asks them to come up with all possible uses for it that they can think of.

"That's easy," says Geoff, a candidate for the position, "Put it on a car's wheels." The interviewer replies, "And what else could you use it for?"
"On a truck's wheels," says Geoff, hesitatingly.
"Anything else?" questions the interviewer.
"I know!" says Geoff, proud of his ingenuity, "A trailer's wheels!"

What limitation underlies Geoff's difficulty with the question?

## USING WHAT YOU HAVE LEARNED

In Chapter 7 you read about how language and thought are interconnected. Many people find it hard even to consider problem solving without the use of language. In fact, some psychologists have stressed the role of self-directed communication in problem solving. Pay attention to your own problem-solving processes. Have you ever found yourself talking to yourself as you go through a problem step by step? Is it more likely to happen when you're all by yourself than with other people? Even if you don't talk out loud to yourself, do you ever talk to yourself "in your head?" Try to imagine thinking or problem solving without the use of language. Can you imagine what thinking might be like for a preverbal infant?

## PART THREE:   TEST AND KNOW
## SAMPLE TEST QUESTIONS

Test how well you have learned this chapter's material by answering the sample test questions.  You may wish to mark your answers on a separate sheet of paper so you can reuse this test for exam review.  Once you have completed the exam, check your answers and then go back to your notes and the textbook to review questions you found difficult.

1.    Mental representations of a class of objects, ideas, or events that share common properties are referred to as

    a.    concepts
    b.    mental images
    c.    mental models
    d.    prototypes

2.    The concept "adult" is a good example of a(n)

    a.    prototype
    b.    fuzzy concept
    c.    basic level category
    d.    implicit category

3.    A prototype is

    a.    a visual representation, such as an image or a geometric form
    b.    a representation of a system that enables people to describe, explain, and predict the way things work
    c.    a mental representation of a class of objects, ideas, or events that share common properties
    d.    an abstraction across many instances of a category

4.    Referring to robins, blue jays, and penguins as "animals" is an example of

    a.    the basic level of categorization
    b.    the superordinate level of categorization
    c.    the defining features method of categorization
    d.    the prototype-matching method of categorization

5.    "The car has started making a funny noise since yesterday.
    Yesterday, I filled the tank with that new "gasohol" for the first time.
    It must be that new "gasohol" that is responsible for the funny noise."

    This reasoning is an example of

    a.    problem solving
    b.    hypothesis testing
    c.    inductive reasoning
    d.    deductive reasoning

6.    Your friend's mother claims that she was unable to program the VCR to record a favorite TV program until it was explained to her in terms of how she usually programs the microwave to cook a chicken while she is at work. This is an example of

    a.    deductive reasoning
    b.    analogical reasoning
    c.    syllogistic reasoning
    d.    inductive reasoning

7.    Dave and Nancy sent out 100 invitations to their wedding. They then took the number of replies they received and multiplied them by the price per plate that the caterer had given, to arrive at the cost of the wedding reception dinner. This problem-solving strategy is an example of a(n)

    a.    algorithm
    b.    syllogism
    c.    heuristic
    d.    prototype

8.    The process of weighing the pros and cons of different alternatives before making a choice is called

    a.    hypothesis testing
    b.    decision making
    c.    inductive reasoning
    d.    deductive reasoning

9.    When the fan belt broke on her car, Melanie pulled out a pair of nylons from her shopping bag and told John "This will fix it!" John just couldn't see how you could use nylons for anything other than wearing. John's problem is known as

    a.    the representativeness heuristic
    b.    the availability heuristic
    c.    the confirmation bias
    d.    functional fixedness

10.    After spending the morning trying to solve a problem, Mazen decided to forget about it. That night, while lying in bed, the answer suddenly came to him. This is an example of

    a.    implicit problem solving
    b.    reasoning by analogy
    c.    deductive reasoning
    d.    decision making

11.    Connectionist models differ from traditional information-processing models in that the underlying metaphor is no longer really "mind as computer." Rather it is mind as

    a.    algorithm
    b.    heuristic
    c.    brain
    d.    programmer

12. Damage to the _____ is associated with impaired planning, distractibility, and deficits in working memory.

   a.    dorsolateral prefrontal cortex
   b.    ventrolateral prefrontal cortex
   c.    ventromedial prefrontal cortex
   d.    all of the above

13. The suffix "s," added to a noun to make it plural, is an example of

   a.    a phoneme
   b.    a constituent
   c.    a morpheme
   d.    transformational grammar

14. The language development of children raised in extreme isolation

   a.    provides evidence for the nonverbal communication hypothesis
   b.    provides evidence for the critical period hypothesis
   c.    typically surpasses that of non-isolated children because of the lack of distracters in their environment
   d.    provides evidence for the behaviorist view of language acquisition

15. Most English-speaking 4-year-olds use the reflexive pronoun "hisself" instead of the correct "himself." This tendency

   a.    is evidence of phonemic restoration
   b.    is evidence of how "motherese" affects language acquisition
   c.    raises questions concerning the notion that there is a "critical period" for language acquisition
   d.    can be viewed as evidence against the behaviorist explanation of language acquisition

16. Chomsky argued that humans are born with what he called a _____ device, an innate set of neural structures for acquiring language.

   a.    syntactical processing
   b.    language processing
   c.    grammatical awareness
   d.    language acquisition

17. Nine-month-old Tammy frequently says "dada." This is an example of

   a.    motherese                  b.    telegraphic speech
   c.    babbling                    d.    fatherese

18. All of the following are characteristics of motherese, *except*

   a.    fast rate of speech
   b.    exaggerated intonation
   c.    slow rate of speech
   d.    high pitch

19. Children whose parents are deaf

   a.    are delayed in language development, which lags behind other aspects of their cognitive development
   b.    are no different in language acquisition from those of hearing parents, unless the children are deaf as well
   c.    are delayed in both language and cognitive development
   d.    are usually both deaf and language-delayed

20. Twenty-month-old Manal points to the fridge and says, "Baby want milk." This is an example of

   a.    babbling
   b.    telegraphic speech
   c.    the language acquisition device
   d.    the Whorfian hypothesis

# ANSWERS

## FILL-IN EXERCISES

1. thinking  2. mental models  3. basic; superordinate  4. reasoning  5. inductive reasoning  6. analogical reasoning  7. initial; goal; operators  8. utility; probability  9. availability  10. implicit  11. ventromedial  12. language; thought  13. procedural  14. content; grammar  15. telegraphic  16. critical period

## APPLICATION

1. inductive reasoning; confirmation bias
2. deductive reasoning
3. availability heuristic
4. functional fixedness

## SAMPLE TEST QUESTIONS

| 1. | a | 11. | c |
|----|---|-----|---|
| 2. | b | 12. | a |
| 3. | d | 13. | c |
| 4. | b | 14. | b |
| 5. | c | 15. | d |
| 6. | b | 16. | d |
| 7. | a | 17. | c |
| 8. | b | 18. | a |
| 9. | d | 19. | a |
| 10. | a | 20. | b |

# Chapter 8
# INTELLIGENCE

## PART ONE: PRE-READ AND WORK
## OUTLINE AND LEARNING OBJECTIVES

Pre-read this chapter's table of contents and end-of-chapter summary. Then, use the outline segment-by-segment to help you work through the chapter. Jot down your own questions, comments, and notes in the space provided. Make a note of difficult areas that you will need to review (include page numbers). Then, answer the questions in the learning objectives section that follows. Check off those you are confident that you can answer well. Re-read the material in the text for the questions about which you are less confident. Record the important points from your reading in the space below each question.

## OUTLINE

I. THE NATURE OF INTELLIGENCE

   A. Intelligence is Multifaceted and Functional

   B. **A Global Vista:** The Cultural Context of Intelligence

II. INTELLIGENCE TESTING

   A. Binet's Scale

   B. Intelligence Testing Crosses the Atlantic

   C. Validity and Limitations of IQ tests

### III.   APPROACHES TO INTELLIGENCE

A. The Psychometric Approach

B. The Information-Processing Approach

C. A Theory of Multiple Intelligences

### IV.   HEREDITY AND INTELLIGENCE

A. Individual Differences in IQ

B. Group Differences: Race and Intelligence

C. **Commentary:** The Science and Politics of Intelligence

### V.   THE EXTREMES OF INTELLIGENCE

A. Mental Retardation

B. Giftedness

C. Creativity and Intelligence

D. **From Mind to Brain:** Creativity and Mental Disorders

## VI.  SOME CONCLUDING THOUGHTS

## LEARNING OBJECTIVES

Upon completion of Chapter 8, you should be able to answer the following questions.

1.    What four questions are central to understanding intelligence?

2.    Explain how intelligence can be viewed as culturally defined.

3.    How did the efforts of Alfred Binet differ from those of Sir Francis Galton in measuring the intelligence of an individual?

4.    What is meant by the concept of mental age, introduced by Binet and Simon in 1908?

5.    On the Stanford-Binet Scale (1916), how was an intelligence quotient (IQ score) calculated?

6.    What were David Wechsler's contributions to modern-day intelligence testing procedures?

7.    What are the criticisms and controversies that have surrounded IQ testing?

8.    Discuss the issue of whether IQ tests are culturally biased.

9.    What are Spearman's two factors, and how are they related to one another?

10.    How do fluid intelligence and crystallized intelligence differ?

11.    What are some of the limitations of the psychometric approach to intelligence?

12.    How would a cognitive psychologist, from the information-processing approach, define intelligence?

13.    What three processes underlie performance on intelligence tests, as identified by researchers studying cognitive processes?

14.    What is the major limitation of the information-processing approach to intelligence?

15.    What are the seven intelligences identified by Howard Gardner? What criteria did he employ in choosing them?

16.    What are the strengths and limitations of the theory of multiple intelligences?

17.    What have findings of twin, family, and adoptions studies shown about the influence of nature and nurture on intelligence?

18.    Outline Arthur Jensen's hypothesis concerning race and intelligence. What has research testing this hypothesis shown?

19.    What are the possible causes of both mental retardation and giftedness?

20.    What is the process of normalization of mentally retarded individuals? Describe the controversy that has surrounded this process.

21.    How is creativity related to intelligence, giftedness, and mental disorders?

22.    How is creativity typically measured?

## PART TWO:    REVIEW AND LEARN
## KEY TERMS, FILL-IN EXERCISES, APPLICATION AND USING WHAT YOU HAVE LEARNED

Before doing the exercises below, review the information you learned in this chapter. Reread the work you did in part one of this study guide chapter, plus the interim summaries and end-of-chapter summary in your textbook.  Review any problem areas.  Once you feel comfortable with the material, do the following exercises without referring to your notes or textbook. If you have difficulty with a term or question, mark it and come back to it. When you have finished an exercise, go back to your notes and the textbook to find the answers to the questions that gave you difficulty.  Finally, check your answers (key terms against the textbook and the rest against the answer key).

## KEY TERMS

Upon completion of Chapter 8, you should be able to define the following terms.

Intelligence  _____

_____

Psychometric instruments _____

_____

Intelligence tests    _____

_____

Mental age (MA)    _____

_____

Stanford-Binet scale_____

_____

Intelligence quotient (IQ)  _____

_____

Group tests _____

_____

Wechsler Adult Intelligence Scale-Third Edition (WAIS-III) _____

_____

Wechsler Intelligence Scale for Children-III (WISC-III) _____

_____

Culture-free _____

_____

Psychometric approach _____

_____

Factor analysis _____

_____

Spearman's two-factor theory _____

_____

g-factor _____

_____

s-factor _____

_____

Gf-Gc theory _____

_____

Fluid intelligence _____

_____

Crystallized intelligence _____

_____

Speed of processing _____

_____

Knowledge base _____

_____

Gardner's theory of multiple intelligences _____

_____

Savants _____

_____

Prodigies _____

_____

Mental retardation _____

_____

Down syndrome _____

_____

Phenylketonuria (PKU) _____

_____

Normalization _____

_____

Giftedness _____

_____

Creativity          _____

_____

Divergent thinking _____

_____

Bipolar disorder    _____

_____

Social intelligence _____

_____

## FILL-IN EXERCISES

Fill in the word or words that best fit in the spaces below.

1.  In recent years, psychologists have come to recognize that intelligence is multi-_____, _____, and _____ defined.

2.  From a(n) _____ perspective, people use their intelligence to satisfy wishes and avoid things they fear.

3.  For the purpose of intelligence testing, psychologists use _____ instruments; these are psychological tests that compare individuals in a population to determine how people differ on certain dimensions.

4.  The most direct ancestor of today's intelligence tests was developed in France, in the year 1905, by _____ _____.

5.  In addition to a single, overall IQ score, the WAIS-III yields separate scores for each of the 14 subtests and overall scores for _____ and _____ intelligence.

6.  David Wechsler is credited with remedying the problems associated with the concept of *mental age* by abandoning the concept, and, instead, calculating IQ as an individual's position relative to peers of the same age on a _____ _____.

7.  The _____ of any psychological test (including an intelligence test) refers to its ability to measure the construct it is attempting to assess.

8. The primary tool of the psychometric approach to intelligence is _____ _____, a statistical procedure for identifying common elements that underlie performance on a wide variety of measures.

9. According to the information-processing approach, intelligence is best defined as a _____ rather than as a measurable quantity; individual differences in intelligence are assumed to reflect differences in the _____ operations people use in thinking.

10. Howard Gardner's theory of _____ intelligences firmly grounds intelligence in both its _____ and cultural context.

11. The logic of _____, _____, and _____ studies in distinguishing the impact of nature and nurture on intelligence is to examine subjects whose approximate degree of genetic relatedness is known and then to correlate the degree of genetic relatedness with measured IQ.

12. The results of the Texas Adoption Project support the findings of other studies that both genetics and environment influence IQ in childhood, but that the impact of the social environment _____ with age, as the impact of genetics _____.

13. Roughly 2% of the American population is _____ _____, that is, significantly subaverage in general intellectual functioning, with deficits in adaptive behavior evident during childhood.

14. Persons whose IQs fall on the extreme _____-hand side of the bell-shaped IQ distribution are generally classified as gifted.

15. _____ is a quality that is related to both intelligence and giftedness; this quality can be defined as "the ability to produce valued outcomes in a novel way."

16. Intelligence is always at the service of goals, which means that it is embedded in a psychological context that includes both _____ and _____.

## APPLICATION

1. A friend of yours has just watched a television talk show that focused on the IQ and race controversy. This is the first time your friend has ever heard about IQ differences between racial groups, and the whole issue has left her rather confused. Knowing that you're studying the topic of intelligence in your psychology course, she turns to you to provide answers to some of her questions.

Her major question is whether intelligence is inherited or is the consequence of the environment in which a person grows up. Drawing on findings from twin, family, and adoption studies that you've read about in Chapter 8, what would you tell her concerning the relative roles of heredity and environment in both individual and group differences in IQ?

2. A friend who is a parent has just been told that her child has been identified as "*gifted*." She has lots of questions about what giftedness means. Because she knows that you've been studying the topic of intelligence, your friend asks what you can tell her about giftedness. She wonders whether giftedness is related to IQ. She's also heard, however, that giftedness has something to do with creativity and wonders how IQ and creativity may be related. Finally, she's heard stories that gifted children may grow up unhappy and socially maladjusted. From what you've read in Chapter 8, how would you answer her questions and concerns?

3. Two psychology students are discussing the criticism that IQ tests may be culturally biased. After examining sample questions from several popular IQ tests, they conclude that the biggest problem is questions that are heavily language-based and assess general knowledge. They propose developing a "*culture-free*" test that does not require language and does not assess general knowledge. Instead, their test would measure intelligence in terms of how quickly people can sort abstract geometrical shapes. They're convinced that their test couldn't possible be culturally biased. Based on what you've read in Chapter 8, do you agree? Why or why not?

## USING WHAT YOU HAVE LEARNED

A senior in high school, Jeffrey almost didn't come to school today, at all. This morning his parents dropped a bombshell: They're getting a divorce! Coming as a complete shock, this news had a profound effect on Jeffrey, making him upset, confused, and sad. It's as if all of a sudden his whole world has been turned upside down. To make matters worse, today is the day that the Scholastic Aptitude Test (SAT) is being administered at Jeffrey's school. Being a straight A student, Jeffrey plans to attend college in the fall. His marks on the SAT will, to a large extent, influence whether or not he will be accepted into the college of his choice.

If you were a close friend of Jeffrey would you recommend that he write the SAT today? Why or why not? If Jeffrey decides to write the SAT, what effect might his present emotional state have on his test scores? If, during the test, Jeffrey is especially anxious to get home and talk things over with his parents, is this likely to make matters worse? Why or why not?

## PART THREE:    TEST AND KNOW
## SAMPLE TEST QUESTIONS

Test how well you have learned this chapter's material by answering the sample test questions. You may wish to mark your answers on a separate sheet of paper so you can reuse this test for exam review. Once you have completed the exam, check your answers and then go back to your notes and the textbook to review questions you found difficult.

1.    Intelligence is functional. From an evolutionary perspective,

    a.    people use their intelligence to satisfy wishes and avoid things they fear.
    b.    intelligent behavior solves problems of adaptation and hence facilitates survival and reproduction.
    c.    intelligence is applied cognition, using cognitive skills to solve problems or obtain desired ends.
    d.    all of the above.

2.    Western views of intelligence typically emphasize:

    a.    verbal skills, and mathematical and spatial abilities
    b.    verbal skills, practical abilities, and competencies
    c.    personal qualities, skills, and cognitive style
    d    independence, alertness, and verbal skills

3.    History will remember _____, not only as the first to attempt to test mental abilities, but also as a pioneering statistician who first expressed the relationship between two variables using (the) _____ _____, which is an important statistical tool in understanding intelligence.

    a.    Galton; correlation coefficient    b.    Binet; correlation coefficient
    c.    Binet; factor analysis    d.    Spearman; factor analysis

4.    As proposed by Lewis Terman, which of the following formulas *correctly* expresses the intelligence quotient (IQ) as the relation between an individual's mental age (MA) and chronological age (CA) ?

    a.    $IQ = (MA/CA) \div 100$    b.    $IQ = (CA/MA) \div 100$
    c.    $IQ = (MA/CA) \times 100$    d.    $IQ = (CA/MA) \times 100$

5.    If the question "Who wrote Romeo and Juliet?" were asked as part of the WAIS-III, it would most likely be included as an item in the _____ subtest.

    a.    Vocabulary    b.    Performance
    c.    Comprehension    d.    Information

6.  As determined by intelligence tests, IQ is _____ related to school grades, showing a correlation coefficient of between _____ and _____.

    a.  mildly; .60, .70
    b.  strongly; .90, 1.0
    c.  strongly; .60, .70
    d.  mildly; .12, .20

7.  For many years, critics have argued that intelligence tests

    a.  lack a theoretical basis
    b.  fail to capture the type of practical intelligence involved in achieving goals in every day life
    c.  are culturally biased
    d.  all of the above

8.  IQ tests place individuals on a continuum of intelligence, but, in general, they do *not*

    a.  provide an overall IQ score
    b.  explain what intelligence is
    c.  quantify intellectual functioning in a way that allows comparison among individuals
    d.  predict school success

9.  Spearman's theory of intelligence

    a.  attempts to explain the specific cognitive processes that underlie intelligent behavior
    b.  dates back to 1857
    c.  distinguishes the g-factor, or general intelligence, from s-factors, or specific abilities
    d.  contends that highly intelligent people do not tend to be maladjusted

10. The Gf-Gc theory distinguishes two general factors of _____ and _____ intelligence.

    a.  verbal; performance
    b.  fluid, crystallized
    c.  general; specific
    d.  all of the above

11. In contrast to the psychometric approach, which tries to _____ basic abilities, the information-processing approach tries to understand the specific _____ that underlie intelligent behavior.

    a.  complicate; attitudes
    b.  adapt; structure
    c.  quantify; processes
    d.  none of the above

12.    Which of the following three variables have been identified by information-processing theorists as being particularly important in explaining individual differences in intelligence?

   a.    speed of processing; memory strategies; socioeconomic status
   b.    knowledge base; cultural heritage; ability to acquire/apply mental strategies
   c.    memory strategies; socioeconomic status; divergent thinking patterns
   d.    speed of processing; knowledge base; ability to acquire/apply mental strategies

13.    Gardner's theory of multiple intelligences distinguishes seven kinds of intelligence that are

   a.    relatively dependent and neurologically indistinct, and show similar courses of development
   b.    relatively independent and neurologically distinct, and show different courses of development
   c.    relatively independent and neurologically distinct, and show similar courses of development
   d.    relatively dependent and neurologically indistinct, and show different courses of development

14.    Which of the following was *not* identified as a type of intelligence by Howard Gardner in his theory of multiple intelligences?

   a.    reasoning
   b.    logical/mathematical
   c.    musical
   d.    bodily/kinesthetic

15.    A longitudinal study examining the relation between a child's IQ at age 4 and 13 and the number of risk factors to which the child was exposed showed that:

   a.    the child's IQ varied directly with the number of risk factors: the more risk factors, the higher the child's IQ
   b.    the number of risk factors to which the child was exposed was unrelated to the child's IQ
   c.    the child's IQ varied inversely with the number of risk factors: the more risk factors, the lower the child's IQ
   d.    environmental variables have little or no effect on individual differences in intelligence

16. In the United States, approximately what percentage of mentally retarded individuals are classified as severely to profoundly retarded?

    a. 2 %
    b. 75 to 90%
    c. 1% or less
    d. 10%

17. More than 70% of mental retardation cases, mostly those in the mild to moderate range, are:

    a. not diagnosed at birth
    b. related to a genetic abnormality, as with Down syndrome and phenylketonuria (PKU)
    c. diagnosed at birth
    d. diagnosed during pregnancy through genetic testing of the amniotic fluid that surrounds the fetus

18. In Western society, with its emphasis on academic aptitude as measured by psychometric tests, giftedness is most often equated with

    a. an IQ that is above average
    b. an IQ exceeding 130
    c. an IQ exceeding 200
    d. creativity

19. One strategy for assessing creativity is to measure _____ thinking. This type of thinking involves generating multiple possibilities from a given situation, such as describing all the possible uses of a coffee cup.

    a. fluid
    b. functional
    c. divergent
    d. cyclothymic

20. Researchers investigating the relation between creativity and mental illness have found that

    a. levels of creativity in the general population are roughly the same as they are among relatives of people with bipolar disorder and people with a mild variant of the disorder
    b. the highest rates of creativity occur in cyclothymic individuals and among relatives of cyclothymic or bipolar individuals
    c. the lowest rates of creativity occur in cyclothymic individuals and among relatives of cyclothymic or bipolar individuals
    d. none of the above

# ANSWERS

## FILL-IN EXERCISES

1. faceted; functional; culturally   2. psychodynamic   3. psychometric   4. Alfred Binet
5. verbal; performance   6. frequency distribution   7. validity   8. factor analysis
9. process; cognitive   10. multiple; neurological    11. twin, family, adoption
12. decreases; increases   13. mentally retarded   14. right   15. creativity
16. motivation; emotion

## APPLICATION

1. Twin, family, and adoption studies show that *both* heredity and environment play important roles in influencing intelligence. While genetic factors may account for many of the observed individual differences in IQ, environmental factors likely account for differences between groups. The analogy of differences in the size of military uniforms from different eras helps explain these differences.

2. Giftedness is frequently defined as IQ exceeding 130; however, several studies have found little correlation between IQ scores and later recognition in such areas as science, creative writing, or performing arts. Many psychologists now consider giftedness to be domain-specific, often limited to particular abilities. Although creativity is related to intelligence, the correlation is far from perfect. Intelligence in a particular area seems to be a necessary, but not sufficient, condition for creativity. Gifted individuals tend to have average or above-average adjustment, slightly better chances of marital success, and far greater likelihood of achieving vocational success than the general population.

3. The students are incorrect. Both sorting abstract geometric shapes and the emphasis on speed in their test can be culturally biased.

## SAMPLE TEST QUESTIONS

| 1. | b | 11. | c |
| 2. | a | 12. | d |
| 3. | a | 13. | b |
| 4. | c | 14. | a |
| 5. | d | 15. | c |
| 6. | c | 16. | d |
| 7. | d | 17. | a |
| 8. | b | 18. | b |
| 9. | c | 19. | c |
| 10. | b | 20. | b |

# Chapter 9
# CONSCIOUSNESS

## PART ONE:    PRE-READ AND WORK
## OUTLINE AND LEARNING OBJECTIVES

Pre-read this chapter's table of contents and end-of-chapter summary. Then, use the outline segment-by-segment to help you work through the chapter. Jot down your own questions, comments, and notes in the space provided. Make a note of difficult areas that you will need to review (include page numbers). Then, answer the questions in the learning objectives section that follows. Check off those you are confident that you can answer well. Re-read the material in the text for the questions about which you are less confident. Record the important points from your reading in the space below each question.

## OUTLINE

I.    THE NATURE OF CONSCIOUSNESS

    A. Functions of Consciousness

    B. Consciousness and Attention

    C. The Normal Flow of Consciousness

II.   PERSPECTIVES ON CONSCIOUSNESS

    A. The Psychodynamic Unconscious

B. The Cognitive Unconscious

C. **Commentary:** An Integrated View of Consciousness

D. **From Mind to Brain:** The Neuropsychology of Consciousness

## III.   SLEEP AND DREAMING

A. The Nature and Evolution of Sleep

B. Stages of Sleep

B. Three Views of Dreaming

C. Sleep Disorders

## IV.   ALTERED STATES OF CONSCIOUSNESS

A. Meditation

B. Hypnosis

C. **One Step Further:** Is Hypnosis Real?

D. Drug-Induced States of Consciousness

E. **A Global Vista:** Religious Experiences in Cross-Cultural Perspective

V.   SOME CONCLUDING THOUGHTS

## LEARNING OBJECTIVES

Upon completion of Chapter 9, you should be able to answer the following questions.

1.   Discuss the two primary functions of consciousness -- monitoring and controlling.

2.   Discuss the three functions of attention.

3.   How have researchers examined the phenomenon of divided attention?

4.   What is daydreaming?

5.   What have beeper studies found concerning the flow of consciousness?

6.   What are some of the ways in which cultural practices and beliefs can influence the way people organize their conscious experiences?

7.   What are the three mental systems that comprise Freud's definition of consciousness?

8.   What is subliminal perception, and can it be used to motivate consumer behavior?

9.   How do cognitive psychologists view conscious and unconscious processes?

10.   Describe the following neurological disorders that disrupt consciousness: blindsight and amnesia.

11.   What are the effects of extreme sleep deprivation?

12.   Describe each of the four stages of sleep.

13.   How do REM and NREM sleep differ?

14.   What are the similarities and differences in the psychodynamic, cognitive, and biological views of the nature and significance of dreams?

15.   What is the most common sleep disorder? Describe its three forms.

16.    Describe each of the following sleep disorders -- nightmares, night terrors, sleep apnea, and narcolepsy. When does each disorder typically occur?

17.    What is meant by the term "altered states of consciousness"?

18.    What are the characteristics of meditation?

19.    What are the characteristics of hypnosis?

20.    How did Ernest Hilgard discover the hidden observer, and what are the implications of this finding?

21.    What are some of the successful applications of hypnosis in retrieving forgotten memories? What concerns do many psychologists have over this use of hypnosis?

22.    Is hypnosis real? Consider this question from two different perspectives: (a) the perspective of a skeptic, and (b) the perspective of an advocate of hypnosis.

23.    What are the effects of each of the following psychoactive substances?

alcohol and other depressants

stimulants

hallucinogens

marijuana

24.    How do cultural beliefs and personal experiences influence the effects of psychoactive substances?

25.    In what ways might religious experiences be considered altered states of consciousness?

## PART TWO:    REVIEW AND LEARN
## KEY TERMS, FILL-IN EXERCISES, APPLICATION AND USING WHAT YOU HAVE LEARNED

Before doing the exercises below, review the information you learned in this chapter. Reread the work you did in part one of this study guide chapter, plus the interim summaries and end-of-chapter summary in your textbook. Review any problem areas. Once you feel comfortable with the material, do the following exercises without referring to your notes or textbook. If you have difficulty with a term or question, mark it and come back to it. When you have finished an exercise, go back to your notes and the textbook to find the answers to the questions that gave you difficulty. Finally, check your answers (key terms against the textbook and the rest against the answer key).

## KEY TERMS

Upon completion of Chapter 9, you should be able to define the following terms.

Consciousness    _____

_____

Attention    _____

_____

Selective inattention_____

_____

Divided attention  _____

_____

Dichotic listening tasks  _____

_____

Daydreaming  _____

_____

Experience sampling  _____

_____

Beeper Studies  _____

_____

Conscious mental processes  _____

_____

Preconscious mental processes  _____

_____

Unconscious mental processes  _____

_____

Subliminal perception  _____

_____

Cognitive unconscious  _____

_____

Unconscious cognitive processes  _____

_____

Preconscious cognitive processes _____

_____

Blindsight    _____

_____

Circadian rhythm    _____

_____

Stage 1 sleep _____

_____

Stage 2 sleep _____

_____

Stage 3 sleep _____

_____

Stage 4 sleep _____

_____

Delta sleep    _____

_____

Rapid eye movement (REM) sleep    _____

_____

Non-REM (N-REM) sleep _____

_____

Manifest content of a dream    _____

_____

Latent content of a dream _____

_____

Insomnia _____

_____

Hypersomnia _____

_____

Nightmares _____

_____

Night terrors _____

_____

Sleep apnea _____

_____

Narcolepsy _____

_____

Altered states of consciousness _____

_____

Meditation _____

_____

Hypnosis _____

_____

Hypnotic susceptibility _____

_____

Hypermnesia _____

_____

Age regression _____

_____

Hypnotic analgesia _____

_____

Posthypnotic suggestions _____

_____

Psychoactive substances _____

_____

Depressants _____

_____

Barbiturates _____

_____

Stimulants _____

_____

Amphetamines _____

_____

Cocaine _____

_____

Hallucinogens _____

_____

Hallucinations _____

_____

Lysergic acid diethylamide (LSD)_____

_____

Religious experiences _____

_____

Possession trances _____

_____

## FILL-IN EXERCISES

Fill in the word or words that best fit in the spaces below.

1. Two functions of consciousness are readily apparent: consciousness _____ the self and the environment, and it _____ thought and behavior.

2. _____ refers to the process of focusing conscious awareness, providing heightened sensitivity to a limited range of experience requiring more extensive information processing.

3. Turning attention away from external stimuli to internal thoughts and imagined scenarios, referred to as _____, is a major component of the normal flow of consciousness.

4. According to Freud unconscious processes are inaccessible to consciousness because they are _____.

5. Information-processing models generally equate consciousness with _____ memory.

6. Disorders of consciousness, like blindsight and amnesia, can result from _____ _____.

7. Although people differ widely in the amount of sleep they need and the amount they actually get, most report sleeping _____ to _____ hours per night.

8.    A _____ rhythm is a cyclical, sleep-wake biological process.

9.    Stage _____ sleep is marked by the emergence of large, slow, rhythmic delta waves (less than 1 cycle per second).

10.   In the late nineteenth century, _____ _____ was considered the realm of "primitives" and charlatans; Freud, however, argued that it was a legitimate scientific and psychological pursuit.

11.   Freud distinguished between the _____ content, or story line of a dream and the _____ content, or its underlying meaning.

12.   Trauma survivors show an elevated incidence of _____ _____, including nightmares and insomnia.

13.   Nightmares typically occur during _____ sleep, and thus can take place at any time during the night. In contrast, night terrors typically occur during _____ sleep, and hence tend to take place in the first two or three hours of sleep.

14.   Many religions, such as Buddhism, believe that _____ leads to a deepened understanding of reality.

15.   The limits of hypnosis are _____ *(significant/insignificant)* enough that many states in the United States now _____ *(outlaw/allow)* the use of hypnotically induced memories in court testimony.

16.   _____ _____ are drugs that operate on the nervous system to alter mental activity.

17.   Psychoactive substances alter consciousness both _____, by facilitating or inhibiting neural transmission at the synapse, and also _____, through expectations shaped by cultural beliefs.

18.   Contrary to what many people who rely on alcohol to elevate their mood believe, alcohol is actually a _____.

19.   Used since about 500 AD, _____ is one of the most *potent* pleasure-inducing substances, as well as one of the most addictive, ever discovered.

20.   Hallucinogenic drug use in Europe and North America dramatically increased in the 1960s with the discovery of the synthetic hallucinogen, _____.

# APPLICATION

### Situation

Over the last few weeks, a friend of yours has been having a terrible time getting a good night's sleep. She gets to sleep easily enough, but it seems that she wakes up a dozen times or more during the night. Even worse, often times, by about four in the morning, she is so wide awake (and frustrated) that she just *can't* get back to sleep. This situation has been going on for some time, and she's really starting to worry about it. Lately, she's been so worried about not getting a good night's sleep that she can hardly sleep at all.

### Questions to Answer

1.    How would you react to your friend's growing concern that her sleeplessness might be caused by some bigger, more serious health problem?

2.    Based on what you've read about sleep disorders, do you think your friend might be suffering from insomnia? Why or why not? If so, what form of insomnia do you think she might have? What advice would you give her to cope with this condition?

3.    Determined to "sleep-in" on a rainy Saturday morning, your friend makes the decision that -- regardless of the time during the night or the wee hours of the morning that she wakes up -- she will stay in bed, *no matter what*. Is this strategy likely to help her with her problem? Why or why not?

4.    In an effort to *exhaust* herself to sleep, your friend decides that she will attend a late-night high-impact aerobics class, then rush home and go to bed. Is this strategy likely to help her with her problem? Why or why not?

5.    When all else fails, your friend decides that she has no other alternative but to take some of her father's sleeping pills, in order to "put an end to this vicious cycle of sleeplessness, once and for all." What advice would you give her about this decision?

## USING WHAT YOU HAVE LEARNED

On the bus ride home from the state fair, you overhear a young couple in the seat in front of you talking about the "Amazing Alphonso," a hypnotist all of you have just watched perform. The woman is convinced that Alphonso and his show were a hoax; she's sure that most of his "volunteers" were really actors, planted in the audience. The rest, she contends, were just "going along," performing whatever bizarre behaviors Alphonso asked them to -- from barking like a dog to kissing all of the bald men in the audience on the head. As for herself, she's convinced she could *never* be hypnotized!

Having just read about altered states of consciousness, what information might you offer to this woman about the validity of hypnosis? How would you explain the concepts of hypnotic susceptibility and posthypnotic suggestion to her?

Hearing the discussion about the Amazing Alphonso, another passenger on the bus joins in the conversation. Right away, he's recognized as one of the volunteers from the audience who participated in the show! For the last hour, you've watched this man on stage, convinced he was a 6-year-old boy playing at the beach, as he painstakingly built a huge sand castle. When Alphonso walked up and kicked the sand castle over, the man actually cried! Although he is anxious to defend his experience as legitimate, the sand castle builder can remember very little about what went on. He says he was very relaxed, but that he wasn't really conscious of what he was doing. He even acts surprised when he is told about his own behavior and that of his fellow volunteers.

Does the sand castle builder's memory of having been hypnotized seem reasonable? Why or why not? What information might you offer to him about hypnosis? How would you explain the concepts of age regression and the hidden observer?

Now that you've established yourself as the "expert" on hypnosis (on this bus, at least), your fellow passengers want to hear more about what you know. What would you tell them about the use of hypnosis in retrieving forgotten memories? What about its use by police detectives to help solve cases? Finally, how would you summarize the controversy that has surrounded hypnosis?

## PART THREE:   TEST AND KNOW
## SAMPLE TEST QUESTIONS

Test how well you have learned this chapter's material by answering the sample test questions.  You may wish to mark your answers on a separate sheet of paper so you can reuse this test for exam review.  Once you have completed the exam, check your answers and then go back to your notes and the textbook to review questions you found difficult.

1.   Which of the following are able to respond to a stimulus at different levels of consciousness?

   a.   all people
   b.   only individuals suffering from Korsakoff's disorder
   c.   only individuals who have been hypnotized
   d.   only individuals who have ingested psychoactive substances

2.   At any given time, people are dimly aware of

   a.   much more than what is conscious
   b.   only what is conscious
   c.   having certain painful memories repressed
   d.   much less than what is conscious

3.   Splitting attention between two or more tasks is known as

   a.   split-brain attention
   b.   dichotic attention
   c.   selective attention
   d.   divided attention

4.   Alicia is participating in a research study. The experimenter has given her a difficult puzzle to solve; as Alicia works on the puzzle, she has been instructed to talk out loud, "simply reporting the contents of her consciousness." The experimenter records Alicia's verbalizations into categories, such as emotional tone, relatedness to the task at hand, and content. This research design is an example of the _____ technique.

   a.   normal flow
   b.   subliminal priming
   c.   subliminal perception
   d.   experience sampling

5.   Although consciousness occupied a central role in the first textbook on psychology, when behaviorism came into ascendance, the study of consciousness was relegated to the periphery of psychological awareness and remained that way until the

a.   1890s                                        b.   1940s
c.   1980s                                        d.   1960s

6.   As defined by Freud, _____ mental processes are not presently conscious, but could be readily brought to consciousness if the need arose.

a.   subliminal
b.   preconscious
c.   repressed
d.   unconscious

7.   Research into subliminal effects indicates that

a.   the effects of subliminal messages are subtle, cueing existing motives rather than creating new ones
b.   certain types of subliminal messages -- especially backward messages in rock music -- may incite violence
c.   subliminal messages are quite effective in motivating consumer behavior
d.   subliminal messages are in many ways similar to posthypnotic suggestions, motivating people to actions they would not otherwise perform

8.   John Kihlstrom describes _____ cognitive processes as "skills or procedures that operate without awareness and are not accessible to consciousness under any circumstance."

a.   unconscious
b.   preconscious
c.   independent
d.   repressed

9.   Louise has no conscious visual awareness. When shown an object, she denies seeing it, yet she can indicate its location in space or describe its geometric form far better than one would expect simply by chance. Louise is likely suffering from
a.   amnesia.
b.   blindsight.
c.   split brain
d.   Korsakoff's disorder.

10.    People deprived of sleep over the long term

    a.    become more susceptible to illness
    b.    may experience delusions, hallucinations, and paranoid thinking
    c.    may be more susceptible to major alterations in belief and value systems
    d.    all of the above

11.    Which of the following *best* describes the relation between the number of hours that people sleep and mortality rates?

    a.    People who report sleeping for unusually short durations are prone to die earlier than are people who report sleeping eight to nine hours per night.
    b.    People who suffer from disorders of consciousness like blindsight, split brain, and amnesia are prone to die earlier than are people who report sleeping eight to nine hours per night.
    c.    People who report sleeping for unusually long *or* unusually short durations are prone to die earlier than are people who report sleeping in the average range per night.
    d.    People who suffer from sleep disorders like insomnia, hypersomnia, and narcolepsy are prone to die earlier than are people who report sleeping eight to nine hours per night.

12.    When delta waves comprise more than 50 percent of recorded brain activity, a person has entered Stage _____ sleep.

    a.    1
    b.    2
    c.    3
    d.    4

13.    During a typical night's sleep, a complete cycle of REM and NREM sleep occurs about every _____.

    a.    90 minutes
    b.    4 hours
    c.    30 minutes
    d.    hour

14. As proposed by _____, dreams express current concerns of one sort or another, in a language with its own peculiar grammar. For example, the thought, " I am worried about my upcoming exam," might be translated into a dream about falling off a cliff.

a. Freud                    b. Claparede
c. Foulkes                  d. Skinner

15. _____ are/is the most common sleep disorder.

a. Nightmares
b. Insomnia
c. Narcolepsy
d. Night terrors

16. The substance most frequently used by people all over the world to alter their state of consciousness is

a. LSD
b. cocaine
c. alcohol
d. marijuana

17. In the United States, approximately one in _____ people abuse alcohol, and another one in _____ misuse psychoactive substances.

a. five; seven
b. seven; twenty
c. twenty; fifty
d. ten; twenty

18. Which of the following is *not* an example of a stimulant?

a. cocaine
b. nicotine
c. amphetamines
d. alcohol

19. During a _____ high, judgment is moderately impaired, problem solving becomes less focused and efficient, and attention is more difficult to direct; some people also report paranoia or panic symptoms.

a. marijuana                b. PCP
c. Xanax                    d. cocaine

20.    In _____, the soul is believed to be entered by another person or supernatural being.

    a.    meditation
    b.    the "hidden observer" phenomenon
    c.    possession trances
    d.    an LSD high

# ANSWERS

## FILL-IN EXERCISES

1. monitors; controls   2. attention   3. daydreaming   4. repressed   5. working
6. neurological (brain) damage   7. 6.5; 8.5   8. circadian   9. three   10. dream
interpretation   11. manifest; latent   12. sleep disorders   13. REM; delta   14. meditation
15. significant; outlaw   16. psychoactive substances   17. biologically (neurologically);
psychologically   18. sedative (depressant)   19. cocaine   20. lysergic acid diethylamide
(LSD)

## APPLICATION

1. These could be symptoms of depression or trauma, but they could also be simply a
vicious cycle where anxiety over not getting to sleep exacerbates insomnia.
2. Yes, because of her repeated awakenings and early-morning awakenings. She most
likely has middle insomnia and early-morning insomnia. She should establish a regular
bedtime, avoid activities that will produce sympathetic arousal before bedtime, and if
she cannot sleep, get up, rather than roll around endlessly in bed.
3. No, this is not likely to help. The bed becomes a conditioned stimulus for anxiety
resulting from not sleeping, which feeds the insomnia.
4. No, this is not likely to help. This will increase autonomic nervous system arousal
and may aggravate the problem.
5. This could aggravate the problem by interfering with natural sleep cycles.

## SAMPLE TEST QUESTIONS

| 1. | a | 11. | c |
|---|---|---|---|
| 2. | a | 12. | d |
| 3. | d | 13. | a |
| 4. | d | 14. | c |
| 5. | c | 15. | b |
| 6. | b | 16. | c |
| 7. | a | 17. | b |
| 8. | a | 18. | d |
| 9. | b | 19. | a |
| 10. | d | 20. | c |

# Chapter 10
# MOTIVATION

## PART ONE: PRE-READ AND WORK
## OUTLINE AND LEARNING OBJECTIVES

Pre-read this chapter's table of contents and end-of-chapter summary. Then, use the outline segment-by-segment to help you work through the chapter. Jot down your own questions, comments, and notes in the space provided. Make a note of difficult areas that you will need to review (include page numbers). Then, answer the questions in the learning objectives section that follows. Check off those you are confident that you can answer well. Re-read the material in the text for the questions about which you are less confident. Record the important points from your reading in the space below each question.

## OUTLINE

I.   PERSPECTIVES ON MOTIVATION

     A. Evolutionary Perspective

     B. Psychodynamic Perspective

     C. Behaviorist Perspective

     D. Cognitive Perspective

     E. A Hierarchy of Needs

F. Applying the Perspectives on Motivation

G. **A Global Vista:** Cultural Influences on Motivation

## II.  EATING

A. Hunger and Satiety

B. Obesity

C. Eating Disorders

## III.  SEXUAL MOTIVATION

A. The Sexual Response Cycle

B. Nature and Nurture in Sexual Motivation

C. Sexual Orientation

D. **From Mind to Brain:** The Biology of Male Homosexuality

E. Sexual Dysfunctions

IV. PSYCHOSOCIAL MOTIVES

A. Needs for Relatedness

B. Achievement and Other Agency Motives

C. **One Step Further:** Distinguishing the Motives Underlying Achievement

V. SOME CONCLUDING THOUGHTS

## LEARNING OBJECTIVES

Upon completion of Chapter 10, you should be able to answer the following questions.

1. What are the two components of motivation?

2. How does the theory of inclusive fitness account for people's motivation to care for those who are related to them?

3.    What role do pheromones play in communication between organisms?

4.    What two basic drives, according to Freud, motivate human behavior?

5.    How do implicit motives differ from explicit motives?

6.    How are drives and reinforcement related, according to the behaviorist perspective?

7.    How are secondary drives acquired and how do they differ from primary drives?

8.    How do goals serve as motivational variables, according to the cognitive perspective?

9.    Describe five conditions necessary for maximum job performance, according to goal-setting theory.

10.   What are Maslow's five categories of needs and how are they organized?

11.   Describe the three levels of needs that form the basis of ERG theory.

12.   How can culture shape motivation?

13.    How did Cannon and Washburn (1912) illustrate the role of stomach contractions in the perception of hunger?

14.    Explain the glucostatic theory of hunger.

15.    How can obesity be considered culturally relative?

16.    Why is it that dieting may not lead to permanent weight loss?

17.    What role may psychological factors play in obesity?

18.    What are the characteristics of anorexia nervosa and bulimia? How may psychological factors lead to these disorders?

19.    Outline the four phases of the sexual response cycle.

20.    How does the sexual response cycle of females differ from that of males?

21.    What insight do androgenital syndrome and androgen insensitivity syndrome provide into the role of hormones in determining sexual behavior?

22.    Describe the research suggesting hormonal and neuroanatomical differences between homosexual and heterosexual men.

23.    How may maternal stress and genetics account for physiological differences between homosexuals and heterosexuals?

24.    What are the most common forms of sexual dysfunction?

25.    What roles may both physiological and psychological factors play in the development of sexual dysfunction?

26.    Why are needs for relatedness -- such as attachment, intimacy, and affiliation -- important?

27.    How do people with a high need for achievement characteristically behave?

28.    How do performance goals and learning goals affect an individual's response to failure?

29.    How is need for achievement related to both parental and cultural expectations?

## PART TWO:    REVIEW AND LEARN
## KEY TERMS, FILL-IN EXERCISES, APPLICATION AND USING WHAT YOU HAVE LEARNED

Before doing the exercises below, review the information you learned in this chapter. Reread the work you did in part one of this study guide chapter, plus the interim summaries and end-of-chapter summary in your textbook.  Review any problem areas. Once you feel comfortable with the material, do the following exercises without referring to your notes or textbook.  If you have difficulty with a term or question, mark it and come back to it.  When you have finished an exercise, go back to your notes and the textbook to find the answers to the questions that gave you difficulty.  Finally, check your answers (key terms against the textbook and the rest against the answer key).

## KEY TERMS

Upon completion of Chapter 10, you should be able to define the following terms.

Motivation _____

_____

Instincts _____

_____

Inclusive fitness _____

_____

Homeostasis _____

_____

Feedback _____

_____

Set point _____

Wishes _____

_____

Fears _____

_____

Thematic Apperception Test (TAT) _____

_____

Drive reduction theories _____

_____

Primary drives _____

_____

Secondary drives _____

_____

Goal _____

_____

Goal-setting theory _____

_____

Expectancy-value theories _____

_____

Hierarchy of needs _____

_____

Self-actualization needs _____

_____

Deficiency needs _____

_____

Growth needs _____

_____

ERG theory _____

_____

Metabolism _____

_____

Absorptive phase _____

_____

Fasting phase _____

_____

Glucostatic theory of hunger _____

_____

Glucoreceptors _____

_____

Obesity _____

_____

Set-point theory _____

_____

Anorexia nervosa _____

_____

Bulimia _____

_____

Sexual response cycle _____

_____

Excitement phase _____

_____

Plateau phase _____

_____

Orgasm _____

_____

Resolution phase _____

_____

Organizational effects _____

_____

Androgenital syndrome _____

_____

Androgen insensitivity syndrome _____

_____

Activational effects _____

_____

Sexual orientation _____

_____

Sexual dysfunctions _____

_____

Psychosocial motives _____

_____

Relatedness _____

_____

Agency _____

_____

Attachment motivation _____

_____

Intimacy _____

_____

Affiliation _____

_____

Need for achievement _____

_____

Performance goals _____

_____

Performance-avoidance goals _____

_____

Mastery goals _____

_____

## FILL-IN EXERCISES

Fill in the word or words that best fit in the spaces below.

1.    Motivation is comprised of the following two components:  the _____ in which the activity is motivated and the _____ of the motivation.

2.    _____ are fixed patterns of behavior that animals produce without learning.

3.    _____ refers to the body's tendency to maintain a relatively constant state that permits cells to live and function.

4.    Freud proposed that the two basic drives underlying human behavior are _____ and _____. Contemporary psychodynamic theorists, however, emphasize two other motives: the need for _____ to others and the need for _____-_____.

5.    Contemporary psychodynamic theorists focus more on _____ and _____ than on drives.

6.    The Thematic Apperception Test tends to evoke _____ motives, whereas self-report activates _____ motives.

7.    According to the behaviorist view, unfulfilled needs lead to _____.

8.    Cognitive researchers often focus on _____ (desired outcomes established through social learning) as a motivational construct.

9.    A cognitive theory of motivation used widely by organizational psychologists interested in worker motivation is goal-_____ theory.

10.    Abraham Maslow proposed that needs are organized according to a _____.

11.    ERG theory condenses the needs described by Maslow to the following three levels: _____, _____, and _____.

12.    Erich Fromm argued that a culture's socioeconomic system shapes people's motivations so that they _____ to act in ways that the system _____ them to act.

13.    Both the liver and the hypothalamus contain _____ , cells that monitor glucose levels.

14.   The tastiness or appeal of food, referred to as _____, is an external factor that serves as a motivator to eat.

15.   Obesity is defined as body weight that is _____ % or more above the ideal for one's height and age.

16.   _____-_____ theory suggests that each person has a natural weight to which the body gravitates, regulated by the hypothalamus.

17.   Bulimia is characterized by a _____-and-_____ syndrome.

18.   During the _____ phase of the sexual response cycle, the person's physiological and psychological functioning gradually returns to normal.

19.   In contemporary Western society, approximately _____ to _____ % of men and _____ % of women consider themselves homosexual.

20.   Two major clusters of psychosocial goals pursued cross-culturally are _____ (or communion) and _____ (achievement, mastery, power, and other self-oriented goals).

## USING WHAT YOU HAVE LEARNED

For some time, it has been known that cigarette smoking is linked to a host of serious medical problems, including increased risk of cardiac problems, emphysema, circulatory problems, and especially lung cancer. The risks inherent in smoking are well-publicized. There are anti-smoking ads on TV and in other media. As well, speakers address teenagers in high school, exhorting them not to begin smoking or, if they already have, to quit smoking. The percentage of the population that smokes has declined significantly. Yet many teenagers still take up smoking. In fact, there has been an increase lately in the number of teenage girls who take up smoking.
A national committee has been formed to investigate the causes of teenage smoking. You have been appointed to the committee, because it is well known that you are able to understand motivation from multiple perspectives. The committee turns to you for a brief report on what might underlie the apparently self-destructive behavior of teenagers who take up smoking. They want to attack this problem from as many angles as possible and ask you to "cover all the bases," theoretically. Referring to as many perspectives as possible, how would you explain people continuing to smoke, despite the risk? What suggestions would you offer to deal with this problem?

## APPLICATION

### Situation

Two of your friends are engaged in a heated discussion about obesity. One argues that obesity is the biggest preventable health problem after smoking. She believes that obese people need to use only a little self-control and reduce their calorie intake to control their weight problem. The other student agrees and adds that, as far as she's concerned, the "majority" of women are overweight. The two students agree and go on to talk about how "lazy," unattractive, and socially inept overweight people are.

Having just studied the topic of motivation, you feel you are in a position to offer some informed input. Based on what you have read, address the following points.

### Questions to Answer

1.    To what extent is obesity a health problem?

2.    Is it true that the majority of women are overweight? What is the medical definition of obesity? Approximately what proportion of the adult American population is obese?

3.    Could the student's view that the "majority" of women are overweight be culturally biased? How would someone have responded in an earlier time or perhaps in a non-western culture?

4.    How would you respond to the students' statements about the laziness, attractiveness, and social skills of overweight people?

5.    Is it true that all that's needed is willpower and dieting? How could you explain to these students that the issue is more complicated than they think (Hint: refer to set-point theory.)

# PART THREE:   TEST AND KNOW
# SAMPLE TEST QUESTIONS

Test how well you have learned this chapter's material by answering the sample test questions. You may wish to mark your answers on a separate sheet of paper so you can reuse this test for exam review. Once you have completed the exam, check your answers and then go back to your notes and the textbook to review questions you found difficult.

1.    The primary motivations that emerge in cross-cultural research are

    a.    power; love        b.    relatedness to others; self-esteem
    c.    sex; aggression       d.    achievement; intimacy

2.    In addition to sexual and aggressive desires, current psychodynamic theorists emphasize two other motives:

    a.    power; love        b.    relatedness to others; self-esteem
    c.    sex; aggression       d.    achievement; intimacy

3.    Which of the following can be considered a secondary drive?

    a.    the desire for food        b.    the desire for water
    c.    the desire for money      d.    the desire for sex

4.    At the highest level in Maslow's hierarchy of needs are

    a.    self-actualization needs    b.    safety needs
    c.    belongingness needs       d.    esteem needs

5.    Self-actualization needs differ from other needs in Maslow's hierarchy in that they are

    a.    deficiency needs       b.    esteem needs
    c.    belongingness needs      d.    growth needs

6.    ERG theory condenses Maslow's hierarchy to three levels:

    a.    esteem, relatedness, growth
    b.    existence, reproduction, growth
    c.    existence, resolution, growth
    d.    existence, relatedness, growth

7.    The absorptive phase and fasting phase are the two phases of

a.    the sexual response cycle        b.    the glucostatic theory of hunger
c.    metabolism                       d.    palatability

8.    A disorder in which the person gorges on food and then either induces vomiting or uses laxatives is

a.    obesity                          b.    anorexia nervosa
c.    bulimia                          d.    androgenital syndrome

9.    What percentage of anorexics are male?

a.    10%                              b.    25%
c.    50%                              d.    75%

10.    Maximum arousal occurs during which phase of the sexual response cycle?

a.    resolution                       b.    plateau
c.    orgasm                           d.    excitement

11.    The final phase of the sexual response cycle is

a.    resolution                       b.    orgasm
c.    plateau                          d.    excitement

12.    A disorder in which the adrenal glands secrete too much androgen in utero, masculinizing the genitals in females, is

a.    androgenital syndrome
b.    androgen insensitivity syndrome
c.    maternal stress syndrome
d.    anorexia nervosa

13.    Unless hormones called _____ are present, all human fetuses develop into _____.

a.    estrogens; males                 b.    androgens; males
c.    androgens; females               d.    estrogens; females

14.    The direction of a person's enduring sexual attraction is referred to as

a.    sexual preference                b.    sexual response
c.    sexual orientation               d.    sexual motivation

15. The desire for physical and psychological proximity to another person and for the comfort and positive emotion experienced in the person's presence is called

    a.   attachment motivation          b.   need for achievement
    c.   performance goals              d.   intrinsic motivation

16. Women who report having _____ are 10 times less likely to suffer depression following a stressful event than women who do not.

    a.   a confidante                   b.   an active sexual life
    c.   a rewarding career             d.   money

17. People high in need for achievement

    a.   enjoy being challenged and are not worried about failing
    b.   worry so much about failure that they will only undertake tasks if they are assured of success
    c.   tend to take risks because of their insatiable need for challenge
    d.   enjoy being challenged but do not want to fail

18. Bill is studying photography. He's not doing it to get the diploma that comes at the end of his program. Rather, his primary purpose is to become a better photographer. His goal would be described as a

    a.   performance goal
    b.   performance-avoidance goal
    c.   mastery-avoidance goal
    d.   mastery goal

19. Which of the following parenting practices is *not* associated with a high need for achievement?

    a.   discouraging children from complaining
    b.   encouraging children to attempt new tasks well beyond their reach
    c.   encouraging independent thinking
    d.   encouraging children to try new solutions when they encounter failure

20. Examination of the inaugural addresses of American presidents reveals that affiliation and achievement motivation are _____ correlated with historians' ratings of presidential success.

    a.   strongly                       b.   not at all
    c.   inversely                      d.   weakly

# Answers

## Fill-in Exercises

1. direction; strength  2. instincts  3. homeostasis  4. sex, aggression; relatedness, self-esteem  5. wishes; fears  6. implicit (unconscious); explicit (conscious)  7. drives  8. goals  9. setting  10. hierarchy  11. existence, relatedness, growth  12. want; needs  13. glucoreceptors  14. palatability  15. 15  16. set-point  17. binge, purge  18. resolution  19. 2; 7; 1  20. relatedness; agency

## Application

1. Obesity is associated with heart disease, high blood pressure, diabetes, and an increased mortality rate.
2. The majority is not overweight, although the percentage is increasing. Body weight that is 15% above the ideal for one's height and age is the medical definition of obesity. By this criterion, approximately 1/3 of the population in the United states is obese.
3. Yes, their view could be culturally biased. North American culture is preoccupied with thinness. Standards in other cultures or other eras are (were) different. Beauty is associated with bulk in many other cultures.
4. These are stereotypes that can lead to differences in how obese people are treated, which can actually result in less attractive *behavior* on the part of obese people.
5. Each person has a natural weight to which the body gravitates, regulated by the hypothalamus. If a person lowers his or her caloric input through dieting, the body may slow metabolism to maintain the set-point weight in spite of fewer calories. Thus, the more you lose, the harder losing may become.

## Sample Test Questions

| | | | |
|----|---|-----|---|
| 1. | a | 11. | a |
| 2. | b | 12. | a |
| 3. | c | 13. | c |
| 4. | a | 14. | c |
| 5. | d | 15. | a |
| 6. | d | 16. | a |
| 7. | c | 17. | d |
| 8. | c | 18. | d |
| 9. | a | 19. | b |
| 10. | b | 20. | c |

# Chapter 11
# EMOTION, STRESS, AND COPING

**PART ONE:    PRE-READ AND WORK**
**OUTLINE AND LEARNING OBJECTIVES**

Pre-read this chapter's table of contents and end-of-chapter summary.  Then, use the outline segment-by-segment to help you work through the chapter. Jot down your own questions, comments, and notes in the space provided. Make a note of difficult areas that you will need to review (include page numbers). Then, answer the questions in the learning objectives section that follows. Check off those you are confident that you can answer well. Re-read the material in the text for the questions about which you are less confident. Record the important points from your reading in the space below each question.

## OUTLINE

I.    EMOTION

A. Physiological Components

B. Subjective Experience

C. Emotional Expression

D. A Taxonomy of Emotions

E. **From Mind to Brain:** The Neuropsychology of Emotion

F. Emotion Regulation

G. Perspectives on Emotion

H. **One Step Further**: Integrating the Perspectives on Emotion

II.    STRESS

A. Stress as a Psychobiological Process

B. Stress as a Transactional Process

C. Sources of Stress

D. Stress and Health

III.    COPING

A. Coping Mechanisms

B. **A Global Vista:** The Impact of Culture on Coping Styles

C. Social Support

D. **Commentary:** A Caveat About Research on Stress and Coping

## IV.  SOME CONCLUDING THOUGHTS

## LEARNING OBJECTIVES

Upon completion of Chapter 11, you should be able to answer the following questions.

1.  How does the Cannon-Bard theory of emotions differ from the James-Lange theory?

2.  How does emotional disclosure affect health?

3.  How can facial expressions actually influence a person's emotional state?

4.  What are the six facial expressions recognized by people of most cultures?

5.  How do cultures differ in emotional display rules?

6.  What are the differences in how men and women experience and express emotion?

7.    Why is a hierarchical organization perhaps the best approach to classifying emotions?

8.    What are the roles of the hypothalamus, amygdala, and cortex in emotion?

9.    What are the physiological mechanisms underlying two stages of emotional reaction in humans?

10.    How have researchers examined the influence of unconscious emotional processes?

11.    How did Schachter and Singer view the interaction between physiological arousal and cognitive interpretation in emotion?

12.    What role does appraisal play in people's emotional responding?

13.    How can mood influence the encoding and retrieval of information?

14.    How does jealousy differ between males and females, according to the evolutionary perspective?

15.    How can the evolutionary, psychodynamic, behavioral, and cognitive perspectives on emotion be integrated?

16.    How can stress be considered both a psychobiological and a transactional process?

17. What are the three stages of the *general adaptation syndrome* by which the body responds to stressful conditions?

18. How are life events, catastrophes, and daily hassles sources of stress? What are the possible effects of each?

19. How does stress affect the body's capacity to fight illness?

20. Describe the Type-A behavior pattern, in terms of both psychological characteristics and susceptibility to health problems.

21. How is optimism/pessimism related to health?

22. How do problem-focused strategies for coping with stress differ from emotion-focused strategies?

23. How may coping style be considered culturally relative?

24. What are two explanations for the beneficial effects of social support in coping with stress?

## PART TWO:   REVIEW AND LEARN
## KEY TERMS, FILL-IN EXERCISES, APPLICATION AND USING WHAT YOU HAVE LEARNED

Before doing the exercises below, review the information you learned in this chapter. Reread the work you did in part one of this study guide chapter, plus the interim summaries and end-of-chapter summary in your textbook. Review any problem areas. Once you feel comfortable with the material, do the following exercises without referring to your notes or textbook. If you have difficulty with a term or question, mark it and come back to it. When you have finished an exercise, go back to your notes and the textbook to find the answers to the questions that gave you difficulty. Finally, check your answers (key terms against the textbook and the rest against the answer key).

## KEY TERMS

Upon completion of Chapter 11, you should be able to define the following terms.

Emotion (or affect) _____

_____

James-Lange theory _____

_____

Cannon-Bard theory     _____

_____

Alexithymia _____

_____

Emotional expression     _____

_____

Display rules_____

_____

Basic emotions

Positive affect

Negative affect

Emotion regulation

Attributions

Schachter-Singer theory

Mere exposure effect

Stress

General adaptation syndrome

Primary appraisal

Secondary appraisal

Stressors _____

_____

Acculturative stress _____

_____

Catastrophes _____

_____

Daily hassles _____

_____

Immune system _____

_____

B cells _____

_____

T cells _____

_____

Natural killer cells _____

_____

Antibodies _____

_____

Type A behavior pattern _____

_____

Low effort syndrome _____

_____

John Henryism        _____

_____

Coping        _____

_____

Social support        _____

_____

## FILL-IN EXERCISES

Fill in the word or words that best fit in the spaces below.

1.    William James's approach to emotion is also called the _____ theory of emotion.

2.    According to the _____-_____ theory, emotion-inducing stimuli simultaneously elicit both an emotional experience and bodily responses.

3.    An emotion is referred to as _____ if it has characteristic physiological, subjective, and expressive components.

4.    Evidence suggests that _____ *(men/women)* are able to read emotions from other people's faces and nonverbal cues better than _____ *(men/women)*.

5.    Pleasant, approach-related emotions appear to be associated with the _____ frontal cortex, whereas unpleasant, avoidance-related emotions are associated with the _____ frontal cortex.

6.    According to the _____-_____ theory, emotion involves two factors: physiological arousal and cognitive interpretation. Research shows, however, that while _____ may intensify emotional experience, it may not be necessary for an emotion to occur.

7.    From a _____ perspective, emotions often reflect a person's judgment about the extent to which current or potential realities match representations of desired states (wishes) or feared states (fears).

8.   According to Dollar and Miller, the psychodynamic defense mechanism of _____ can actually be considered as an internal mechanism of flight from a thought that would bring an unpleasant feeling.

9.   Stress can be considered both a _____ process and a _____ process.

10.  The organism is especially vulnerable to illness in the _____ stage of the general adaptation syndrome.

11.  Virtually any event that requires someone to make adjustments can be considered a _____.

12.  _____ stress refers to the stress that people experience when trying to adapt to a new culture.

13.  Stressors of massive proportion are referred to as _____.

14.  Individuals who are impatient, hard-driving, ambitious, competitive, and hostile display what is called the _____ behavior pattern.

15.  Changing one's cognition or appraisal of a stressful situation is one method of _____.

## USING WHAT YOU HAVE LEARNED

**How's Your Stress?**

One of the sources of stress you read about in Chapter 11 was life events. With reference to Table 11.2, consider the stressful life events you have confronted over the past 12 months. Do any of them rank high on the list? Have you experienced more than one stressful life event? Can you see how their effects can add up?

How many of the stressors you're dealing with can be considered "challenges," that is, positive changes in your life? Can you see how even positive life events can be stressors?

How do you deal with stress? Do you use physical exercise or relaxation? How about social support? Are you able to talk to another person or people about the life events you're dealing with?

What would you say are the most common stressful life events that university students have to cope with?

# APPLICATION

## Situation

Two students in your psychology class are having a heated debate about how thinking and feeling are related. One argues that how she feels affects what she thinks. She says that when she's feeling down, everything looks negative, while on days when she's feeling really well, she can hardly even remember negative things. The other student agrees that thinking and feeling are related, but argues that it's thinking that affects feeling, and not the other way around. She argues that it's how her friend interprets the situation that leads to feeling down or really good. Who's right?

## Questions to Answer

1.    With reference to the various perspectives on emotion covered in the chapter, discuss how emotion and cognition are related.

2.    Try for yourself to see how cognition and emotion are related. Pay attention to your thoughts and attributions when your mood changes. Does your mood affect your thoughts? Can you influence your emotional state by changing the content of your cognitions?

3.    What role might the physiological components of emotion play in the relation between emotion and cognition?

4.    What role does cognition play in people's emotional reaction to stressful situations? Is there a role for cognition in the coping process?

## PART THREE:    TEST AND KNOW
## SAMPLE TEST QUESTIONS

Test how well you have learned this chapter's material by answering the sample test questions. You may wish to mark your answers on a separate sheet of paper so you can reuse this test for exam review. Once you have completed the exam, check your answers and then go back to your notes and the textbook to review questions you found difficult.

1.    The James-Lange theory of emotion sees the origins of emotion in

    a.    the peripheral nervous system
    b.    the cognitive appraisal of the stressfulness of an event
    c.    the attributions people make concerning their ability to cope
    d.    how we encode and retrieve information about an experience

2.    The correlation between self-reported happiness and prosperity

    a.    is actually negative; money and happiness are inversely related
    b.    is insignificant, regardless of culture or situation
    c.    is substantial within cultures, although minimal across cultures
    d.    is substantial across cultures, although minimal within cultures

3.    In addition to indicating a person's emotional state, facial expressions

    a.    indicate how well she's coping with stress
    b.    tell you what she's thinking
    c.    can indicate what coping mechanisms she's using
    d.    can influence patterns of autonomic response

4.    Cross cultural studies have identified six facial expressions recognized by people of all cultures. These are

    a.    surprise, fear, anger, disgust, happiness, sadness
    b.    anger, fear, curiosity, sadness, contempt, love
    c.    fear, trust, anticipation, love, hate, curiosity
    d.    guilt, shame, fear, anger, joy, friendliness

5.    Children as young as 3 years old recognize that males are more likely than females to express the emotion _____.

    a.    fear            b.    anger
    c.    happiness      d.    sadness

6. Positive and negative affect are

   a.   strongly negatively correlated
   b.   completely uncorrelated
   c.   actually positively correlated, though moderately
   d.   moderately negatively correlated

7. Probably the most important limbic structure for emotion is the

   a.   hypothalamus
   b.   cerebellum
   c.   thalamus
   d.   amygdala

8. The notion that a cognitive judgment or attribution is crucial to emotional experience is central to which theory of emotions?

   a.   James-Lange
   b.   Cannon-Bard
   c.   Schachter-Singer
   d.   Zajonc

9. According to the cognitive perspective, a judgment that a perceived punishment is caused by another person and is unfair results in the emotional response of

   a.   fear
   b.   distress
   c.   anger
   d.   anxiety

10. The finding that subjects more readily recall positive words from a list of words when in a positive mood illustrates that

    a.   positive words are easier to encode and recall than are other words
    b.   negative words are harder to encode and recall than are other words
    c.   mood can affect both encoding and recall of information in memory
    d.   both a and b

11. According to the evolutionary perspective, jealousy in females should focus on

    a.   the male's emotional commitment to other females
    b.   the male's emotional commitment to other males
    c.   the male's sexual relations with other females
    d.   the male's sexual commitment to other females

12.    The three stages of the general adaptation syndrome, by which the body reacts to stress, include

    a.    alarm, arousal, resolution
    b.    alarm, fleeing, fighting
    c.    alarm, plateau, recovery
    d.    alarm, resistance, exhaustion

13.    During the alarm stage of the general adaptation syndrome

    a.    the organism is especially vulnerable to illness
    b.    the body eventually wears down, if the phase lasts long enough
    c.    adrenaline and other hormones are released and the sympathetic nervous system is activated
    d.    all systems may appear to have returned to normal, although the body continues to use its resources at an accelerated rate

14.    According to Richard Lazarus, stress and coping involve two stages. The stage in which a person evaluates her options and determines how to respond is referred to as the

    a.    general adaptation syndrome
    b.    resistance stage
    c.    primary appraisal stage
    d.    secondary appraisal stage

15.    Richard Lazarus distinguishes three types of stress:

    a.    challenge, threat, catastrophes
    b.    threat, harm or loss, challenge
    c.    exhaustion, harm or loss, catastrophes
    d.    hassles, catastrophes, life events

16.    The most stressful of life events, according to the Holmes-Rahe Life Events Rating Scale is

    a.    being fired at work    b.    death of a spouse
    c.    divorce    d.    being jailed

17.    Daily hassles

    a.    in contrast to life events are unlikely to serve as stressors
    b.    are correlated with self-reports of distress and stress-related illnesses
    c.    can easily be coped with using a little denial
    d.    are stressful only for individuals displaying the Type-A behavior pattern

18. The Type-A characteristic that is particularly related to heart disease is

   a. hostility
   b. competitiveness
   c. impatience
   d. ambitiousness

19. John Henryism

   a. is a coping style defined by a tendency to work hard and cope actively despite difficult circumstances
   b. is a coping style characterized by low effort
   c. refers to a two-stage model of stress and coping
   d. is a view of emotion that focuses on the primacy of changes in the peripheral nervous system

20. Social support is an effective resource for coping with stress and involves

   a. being cared for by the state until the person is able to cope on her own again
   b. the presence of others that one can confide in and from whom one can expect help and concern
   c. financial resources provided by social service agencies for people experiencing catastrophic stress
   d. both a and c

# ANSWERS

## FILL-IN EXERCISES

1. peripheral  2. Cannon-Bard  3. basic  4. women; men  5. left; right  6. Schachter-Singer; arousal  7. cognitive  8. repression  9. psychobiological; transactional  10. resistance  11. stressor  12. acculturative  13. catastrophes  14. Type A  15. coping

## SAMPLE TEST QUESTIONS

| | | | |
|---|---|---|---|
| 1. | a | 11. | a |
| 2. | d | 12. | d |
| 3. | d | 13. | c |
| 4. | a | 14. | d |
| 5. | b | 15. | b |
| 6. | d | 16. | b |
| 7. | d | 17. | b |
| 8. | c | 18. | a |
| 9. | c | 19. | a |
| 10. | c | 20. | b |

# Chapter 12
# PERSONALITY

PART ONE:     PRE-READ AND WORK
OUTLINE AND LEARNING OBJECTIVES

Pre-read this chapter's table of contents and end-of-chapter summary. Then, use the outline segment-by-segment to help you work through the chapter. Jot down your own questions, comments, and notes in the space provided. Make a note of difficult areas that you will need to review (include page numbers). Then, answer the questions in the learning objectives section that follows. Check off those you are confident that you can answer well. Re-read the material in the text for the questions about which you are less confident. Record the important points from your reading in the space below each question.

## OUTLINE

I.    PSYCHODYNAMIC APPROACHES

    A. Freud's Models

    B. Neo-Freudians

    C. Object Relations Theory

    D. **One Step Further:** Assessing Unconscious Patterns

    E. Contributions and Limitations of Psychodynamic Approaches

## II.  COGNITIVE SOCIAL THEORIES

### A. Encoding and Personal Relevance

### B. Expectancies and Competences

### C. Self-Regulation

### D. Contributions and Limitations of Cognitive Social Theory

## III.  TRAIT THEORY APPROACHES

### A. Eysenck's Theory

### B. The Five Factor Model

### C. **From Mind to Brain:** The Genetics of Personality

### D. Is Personality Consistent?

E. Contributions and Limitations of Trait Theory

## IV. HUMANISTIC THEORIES

A. Rogers's Person-Centered Approach

B. Existential Approaches to Personality

C. Contributions and Limitations of Humanistic Theories

## V. PERSONALITY AND CULTURE

A. Linking Personality and Culture

B. **A Global Vista:** Interactionist Approaches to Personality and Culture

## VI. SOME CONCLUDING THOUGHTS

## LEARNING OBJECTIVES

Upon completion of Chapter 12, you should be able to answer the following questions.

1.    Explain the differences between the three types of mental processes described by Freud -- the conscious, preconscious, and unconscious.


2.    What role does conflict play in an individual's actions?


3.    What are the major conflicts of each of the following psychosexual stages?

Oral stage

Anal stage

Phallic stage

Latency stage

Genital stage

4.    How is identification linked to the Oedipus complex?


5.    What are the differences between girls and boys in terms of the Oedipus complex?


6.    How do primary process and secondary process thinking differ?


7.    Compare the roles of the id, ego, and superego.


8.    Identify seven defense mechanisms and describe how each functions.

9.    In what ways do the neo-Freudians differ in emphasis from Freud?

10.    What is the focus of object relations theory and how does this approach differ from Freudian theory?

11.    What are the major assessment methods used by psychodynamic psychologists?

12.    What are the major contributions and limitations of psychodynamic theories?

13.    How do cognitive social theories of personality differ from both behaviorist and psychodynamic views?

14.    How does the personal relevance of a situation affect the way individuals process social information and behave interpersonally?

15.    What is the difference between self-efficacy expectancies and competencies? How do these determine the actions people carry out?

16.    What role is played by self-regulation in the execution of behavior?

17.    What is the difference, according to Eysenck's theory, between habits, traits, and types?

18.    Describe the three personality types identified by Eysenck.

19.     Which five superordinate traits make up the *Big Five* factors?

20.     What have studies comparing MZ and DZ twins reared together and apart revealed about the heritability of various personality traits?

21.     Explain Walter Mischel's argument that people do not display traits that are consistent across situations and discuss the arguments against this.

22.     Can it be said that personality traits are consistent over time?

23.     What are the differences between boys and girls in childhood antecedents to depression?

24.     What are four limitations of trait theory approaches to personality?

25.     How does the humanistic approach to personality differ from that of both psychodynamic and cognitive-social theories?

26.     How can interpersonal experiences distort an individual's personality development, according to Carl Rogers's person-centered approach?

27.     What do existentialists mean when they say that people, unlike animals and physical objects,  have no fixed nature and must essentially create themselves?

28.     What are the major contributions and limitations of humanistic approaches to personality?

29. How are personality and culture related in the following four approaches?

Marx's approach

Freud's approach

Culture pattern approach

Interactionist approaches

## PART TWO:  REVIEW AND LEARN
## KEY TERMS, FILL-IN EXERCISES, APPLICATION AND USING WHAT YOU HAVE LEARNED

Before doing the exercises below, review the information you learned in this chapter. Reread the work you did in part one of this study guide chapter, plus the interim summaries and end-of-chapter summary in your textbook. Review any problem areas. Once you feel comfortable with the material, do the following exercises without referring to your notes or textbook. If you have difficulty with a term or question, mark it and come back to it. When you have finished an exercise, go back to your notes and the textbook to find the answers to the questions that gave you difficulty. Finally, check your answers (key terms against the textbook and the rest against the answer key).

## KEY TERMS

Upon completion of Chapter 12, you should be able to define the following terms.

Personality _____

_____

Structure of personality _____

_____

Individual differences _____

_____

Psychodynamics _____

_____

Topographic model _____

_____

Conscious mental processes _____

_____

Preconscious mental processes _____

_____

Unconscious mental processes _____

_____

Ambivalence _____

_____

Conflict _____

_____

Drive model _____

_____

Libido _____

_____

Psychosexual stages _____

_____

Oral stage _____

_____

Anal stage    _____

_____

Phallic stage _____

_____

Latency stage    _____

_____

Genital stage _____

_____

Fixation    _____

_____

Regression    _____

_____

Oedipus complex    _____

_____

Identification    _____

_____

Structural model    _____

_____

Id    _____

_____

Ego    _____

_____

Superego _____

_____

Defense mechanisms _____

_____

Repression _____

_____

Denial_____

_____

Projection _____

_____

Reaction formation _____

_____

Rationalization _____

_____

Passive aggression _____

_____

Neo-Freudians _____

_____

Collective unconscious _____

_____

Archetypes _____

_____

Anima _____

_____

Animus _____

_____

Object relations theory _____

_____

Life history methods _____

_____

Projective tests _____

_____

Rorschach inkblot test _____

_____

Thematic Apperception Test (TAT) _____

_____

Personal constructs _____

_____

Repertory grid technique _____

_____

Personal value _____

_____

Behavior-outcome expectancy _____

_____

Self-efficacy expectancy _____

_____

Competencies _____

_____

Self-regulation _____

_____

Trait _____

_____

Extroversion _____

_____

Neuroticism _____

_____

Psychoticism _____

_____

Big five factors (or Five Factor Model) _____

_____

Person-by-situation interactions _____

_____

Humanistic approaches _____

_____

Person-centered approach _____

_____

Phenomenal experience _____

_____

Empathy _____

_____

True self _____

_____

False self _____

_____

Ideal self _____

_____

Existential theories _____

_____

Existential dread _____

_____

## FILL-IN EXERCISES

Fill in the word or words that best fit in the spaces below.

1. The _____ of personality refers to the way enduring patterns of thought, feeling, and behavior are organized.

2. The ways people differ from one another are referred to as _____ differences.

3. The term _____ refers to conflicting feelings or intentions that affect people's behavior.

4. Freud described the story line of a dream as its _____ content, while its underlying message is its _____ content.

5.    Freud divided mental processes into three types: _____, _____, and _____.

6.    The process of _____ involves making another person part of yourself, trying to become more like the person by adopting his or her attitudes.

7.    The structural model posits three sets of mental forces or structures: _____, _____, and _____.

8.    Jung argued that within all men is a female archetype or _____, just as all women possess an unconscious masculine side or _____.

9.    George Kelly coined the term personal _____ to refer to mental representations of the people, places, things, and events that are significant to a person.

10.   The importance individuals attach to various outcomes or potential outcomes, according to the cognitive social approach, is referred to as _____ value.

11.   According to the cognitive social approach, whether people carry out various actions depends on both expectancies and _____.

12.   A commonly used method of measuring traits involves having people answer questions about themselves by filling out a _____.

13.   Openness to experience, conscientiousness, extroversion, agreeableness, and neuroticism are referred to as the _____ _____ factors by trait theorists.

14.   According to Walter Mischel, _____ variables are more important in determining the way someone acts than are broad personality dispositions.

15.   Shyness and anxiety in the face of novelty is an aspect of temperament referred to by Kagan as _____ to the unfamiliar.

16.   According to Carl Rogers, individuals often wear a mask, which he refers to as a _____ self, which is the result of their natural desire to gain the _____ regard of other people.

17.   The recognition that life has no absolute value or meaning and that ultimately we all face death is a problem referred to as existential _____.

18.   _____ approaches hold that personality, culture, and economics are all interrelated.

## USING WHAT YOU HAVE LEARNED

Identify the individual or approach most closely associated with each of the following concepts.

1.  Big Five factors
2.  Regression
3.  Positive regard
4.  Types
5.  Self-efficacy expectancy
6.  False self
7.  Repertory grid technique
8.  Primary process thinking
9.  Personal constructs
10. Empathy

11. Archetype
12. Self-regulation
13. Extroversion
14. Libido
15. Ideal self
16. Collective unconscious
17. Existential dread
18. Preconscious
19. Personal value
20. Competencies

## APPLICATION

With reference to Freud's psychosexual stages, explain the behavior of each of the following individuals.

1.  Brenda is an extremely insecure woman. She seems to be always concerned with what other people are thinking of her. She has a real need for the approval of others and can't seem to make any decisions on her own. She clings to people, as if she's afraid to let go in case they'll leave her.

2.  Ted is really stingy. He just won't share with anybody. Not only that, he's so concerned that everything be done "just so." You might call him obsessive. Hardly anybody can work with him, because he always insists that everything be done his way.

3.  Mary is the most disorganized person you've ever seen. Her room is an absolute mess. She never completes her assignments, because she always loses them. She's always late for class; in fact, she even missed an exam last term because she overslept.

4.    Bill always has something in his mouth, often a cigarette. Lately, he's been trying to quit smoking by chewing bubble gum (he blows bubbles all the time and pops them, even in class). When he's not smoking or chewing gum, you'll probably find him sucking on a lollipop.

5.    Steve spends all his free time in the gym, working out. He has muscles where most people don't even know there are muscles! When he's not in the gym, he's trying to impress women. It's really important to him that women are attracted to him.

## PART THREE:    TEST AND KNOW
## SAMPLE TEST QUESTIONS

Test how well you have learned this chapter's material by answering the sample test questions. You may wish to mark your answers on a separate sheet of paper so you can reuse this test for exam review. Once you have completed the exam, check your answers and then go back to your notes and the textbook to review questions you found difficult.

1.    Freud proposed two basic drives motivating human behavior:

    a.    sex and aggression
    b.    aggression and violence
    c.    sex and survival
    d.    aggression and destructiveness

2.    The reservoir of sexual and aggressive energy is the

    a.    libido                   b.    ego
    c.    id                     d.    anima

3.    Which of the following is *not* one of Freud's five psychosexual stages?

    a.    navel                b.    anal
    c.    phallic             d.    latency

4.    According to Freud, preconscious mental processes are

    a.    rational, goal-directed thoughts at the center of awareness
    b.    thoughts that are not conscious, but can be retrieved at any time
    c.    irrational, inaccessible thoughts
    d.    inert, unconscious thoughts

5.    Fixations at the latency stage can lead to

   a.    conflicts about giving and receiving
   b.    a preoccupation with attracting mates
   c.    exaggerated needs for approval
   d.    asexuality

6.    Secondary process thinking is characteristic of the

   a.    libido                          b.    ego
   c.    id                              d.    anima

7.    Fixations at the oral stage can lead to

   a.    conflicts about giving and receiving
   b.    a preoccupation with attracting mates
   c.    exaggerated needs for approval
   d.    asexuality

8.    Converting sexual or aggressive impulses into socially acceptable activities involves the defense mechanism of

   a.    denial                          b.    projection
   c.    rationalization                 d.    sublimation

9.    Jung labeled the symbols contained in the collective unconscious:

   a.    anima                           b.    repertories
   c.    apperceptions                   d.    archetypes

10.    Alfred Adler maintained that people are motivated by a lifelong need to

   a.    overcome feelings of inferiority
   b.    fulfill the range of needs that humans experience
   c.    self-actualize
   d.    confront what it means to be human and what values to embrace

11.    Object relations theory explains difficulties people have in maintaining intimate relationships in terms of

   a.    unconscious conflicts
   b.    a natural desire to gain the positive regard of other people
   c.    maladaptive interpersonal patterns laid down in the first few years of life
   d.    the recognition that life has no absolute value or meaning and that ultimately we will all face death

12.    George Kelly and his colleagues developed the _____ to assess individuals' personal constructs indirectly.

    a.    repertory grid technique
    b.    Thematic Apperception Test (TAT)
    c.    Rorschach inkblot test
    d.    person-centered approach

13.    Self-regulation refers to

    a.    setting goals
    b.    evaluating one's performance
    c.    adjusting one's behavior to meet goals
    d.    all of the above

14.    Which of the following is *not* used to measure traits?

    a.    asking people to report on the content of their dreams
    b.    observing people's behavior over time and in different situations
    c.    asking people who know the subject well to fill out questionnaires about the person's personality
    d.    asking people themselves to fill out a self-report questionnaire

15.    Extroversion, neuroticism, and psychoticism are three overarching psychological types identified by

    a.    Kelly
    b.    Rogers
    c.    Eysenck
    d.    Adler

16.    The Big Five factors include

    a.    extroversion, agreeableness, conscientiousness, neuroticism, and openness to experience
    b.    extroversion, agreeableness, conscientiousness, introversion, and openness to experience
    c.    extroversion, inferiority, conscientiousness, neuroticism, and openness to experience
    d.    extroversion, agreeableness, conscientiousness, neuroticism, and ill-temperedness

17. Which of the following is a criticism of trait theory approaches?

   a. They overemphasize the rational side of life and underemphasize the emotional, motivational, and irrational.
   b. They are no more sophisticated than the theories of personality held by lay people.
   c. They have failed to develop a body of testable hypotheses and research.
   d. They are theories aimed at interpretation of behavior that has already occurred, rather than at prediction of behavior.

18. The aim of the psychologist, according to the humanist approach, should be to

   a. understand how individuals experience themselves, others, and the world
   b. search for unconscious conflict that may underlie an individual's behavior
   c. explain behavior in terms of environmental contingencies
   d. explain and alter behavior in terms of contingencies in the "social" environment

19. According to Rogers, the fundamental tool of the psychologist is

   a. the questionnaire
   b. projective tests like the TAT and Rorschach inkblot test
   c. direct observation of an individual across many situations
   d. empathy

20. The notion that people's needs, wishes, beliefs, and values are products of the conditions under which they live and work was proposed by

   a. Karl Marx
   b. Jean-Jacques Rousseau
   c. Jean-Paul Sartre
   d. Harry Stack Sullivan

# ANSWERS

## FILL-IN EXERCISES

1. structure  2. individual  3. ambivalence  4. manifest; latent  5. conscious, preconscious, unconscious  6. identification  7. id, ego, superego  8. anima, animus  9. constructs  10. personal  11. competencies  12. questionnaire  13. Big Five  14. situational  15. inhibition  16. false; positive  17. dread  18. interactionist

## USING WHAT YOU HAVE LEARNED

| | | | |
|---|---|---|---|
| 1. | trait | 11. | psychodynamic (Jung) |
| 2. | psychodynamic (Freud) | 12. | cognitive social |
| 3. | humanistic (Rogers) | 13. | trait (Eysenck) |
| 4. | trait (Eysenck) | 14. | psychodynamic (Freud) |
| 5. | cognitive social (Bandura) | 15. | humanistic (Rogers) |
| 6. | humanistic (Rogers) | 16. | psychodynamic (Jung) |
| 7. | cognitive social (Kelly) | 17. | existential |
| 8. | psychodynamic (Freud) | 18. | psychodynamic (Freud) |
| 9. | cognitive social (Kelly) | 19. | cognitive social |
| 10. | humanistic (Rogers) | 20. | cognitive social |

## APPLICATION

1. oral stage fixation
2. anal stage fixation
3. anal stage fixation
4. oral stage fixation
5. phallic stage fixation

## SAMPLE TEST QUESTIONS

| | | | |
|---|---|---|---|
| 1. | a | 11. | c |
| 2. | c | 12. | a |
| 3. | a | 13. | d |
| 4. | b | 14. | a |
| 5. | d | 15. | c |
| 6. | b | 16. | a |
| 7. | c | 17. | b |
| 8. | d | 18. | a |
| 9. | d | 19. | d |
| 10. | a | 20. | a |

# Chapter 13
# PHYSICAL AND COGNITIVE DEVELOPMENT

## PART ONE: PRE-READ AND WORK
## OUTLINE AND LEARNING OBJECTIVES

Pre-read this chapter's table of contents and end-of-chapter summary. Then, use the outline segment-by-segment to help you work through the chapter. Jot down your own questions, comments, and notes in the space provided. Make a note of difficult areas that you will need to review (include page numbers). Then, answer the questions in the learning objectives section that follows. Check off those you are confident that you can answer well. Re-read the material in the text for the questions about which you are less confident. Record the important points from your reading in the space below each question.

## OUTLINE

I.   BASIC ISSUES IN DEVELOPMENTAL PSYCHOLOGY

    A. Nature and Nurture

    B. The Relative Importance of Early Experience

    C. Stages or Continuous Change?

II.  STUDYING DEVELOPMENT

    A. Cross-Sectional Studies

    B. Longitudinal Studies

B. Piaget's Theory of Cognitive Development

C. The Information-Processing Approach to Cognitive Development

D. Integrative Theories of Cognitive Development

## V.   COGNITIVE DEVELOPMENT AND CHANGE IN ADULTHOOD

A. Studying Cognition and Aging: Some Cautions

B. Cognitive Changes Associated with Aging

C. **Commentary:** Intelligence and Aging

D. Aging and "Senility"

## VI.   SOME CONCLUDING THOUGHTS

## LEARNING OBJECTIVES

Upon completion of Chapter 13, you should be able to answer the following questions.

1.    What is meant by the term critical period? Why is this concept controversial when considering human development?

2.    How does continuous developmental change differ from change that is stage-like?

3.    What are the advantages and disadvantages of three types of research design used by developmental psychologists?

4.    What are the three stages of prenatal development?

5.    What are the prenatal effects of alcohol and crack cocaine?

6.    Compare how the nervous system develops before and after birth.

7.    What differences are there between boys and girls in the effects of early maturation?

8.    What are the major consequences of menopause and how can culture influence women's reactions to this event?

9.    What are the changes in male sexuality that begin at mid-life?

10.    What are the declines in sensory-perceptual functioning commonly associated with aging?

11.    What is "ageism"?

12.    What methods do researchers use to study infant perception and cognition?

13.    Describe the visual and auditory capabilities and preferences of infants.

14.    What has been found concerning intermodal understanding in infants?

15.    What has research shown concerning memory in infants?

16.    How are assimilation and accommodation involved in the process of adaptation to the environment?

17.    What are Piaget's four stages of cognitive development? Indicate the approximate age-range and major characteristics of each stage.

18.    What are four important criticisms of Piaget's theory?

19.    How does the information-processing approach to cognitive development differ from Piaget's approach?

20. Describe the following five important factors that information-processing theorists believe influence children's cognitive efficiency – processing speed, knowledge base, automatic processing, cognitive strategies, and metacognition.

21. How does Case's model integrate Piagetian and information-processing views of cognitive development?

22. Why is the study of cognition and aging complicated?

23. What is "psychomotor slowing" and how can this affect cognitive performance in the elderly.

24. How does memory change in the elderly? What aspects of memory decline with age? What aspects are relatively unaffected by age?

25. In what ways do fluid intelligence and crystallized intelligence differ?

26. What are the characteristics and possible causes of Alzheimer's disease?

## PART TWO:     REVIEW AND LEARN
## KEY TERMS, FILL-IN EXERCISES, APPLICATION AND USING WHAT YOU HAVE LEARNED

Before doing the exercises below, review the information you learned in this chapter. Reread the work you did in part one of this study guide chapter, plus the interim summaries and end-of-chapter summary in your textbook.  Review any problem areas. Once you feel comfortable with the material, do the following exercises without referring to your notes or textbook.  If you have difficulty with a term or question, mark it and come back to it.  When you have finished an exercise, go back to your notes and the textbook to find the answers to the questions that gave you difficulty.  Finally, check your answers (key terms against the textbook and the rest against the answer key).

## KEY TERMS

Upon completion of Chapter 13, you should be able to define the following terms.

Developmental psychology     _____

_____

Maturation     _____

_____

Critical period     _____

_____

Sensitive period     _____

_____

Stage     _____

_____

Cross-sectional study     _____

_____

Cohort effects _____

_____

Longitudinal study _____

_____

Sequential study _____

_____

Prenatal period _____

_____

Germinal period _____

_____

Embryonic period _____

_____

Fetal period _____

_____

Teratogens _____

_____

Fetal alcohol syndrome _____

_____

Rooting reflex _____

_____

Sucking reflex _____

_____

Puberty _____

_____

Menopause _____

_____

Presbycusis _____

_____

Gerontologist _____

_____

Ageism _____

_____

Orienting reflex _____

_____

Intermodal processing _____

_____

Infantile amnesia _____

_____

Assimilation _____

_____

Schema _____

_____

Accommodation _____

_____

Equilibration _____

_____

Sensorimotor stage _____

_____

Operations _____

_____

Object permanence _____

_____

Egocentric _____

_____

Preoperational stage _____

_____

Three-mountain task _____

_____

Centration _____

_____

Concrete operational stage _____

_____

Conservation _____

_____

Formal operational stage _____

_____

Knowledge base _____

_____

Automatization _____

_____

Metacognition _____

_____

Neo-Piagetian theorists _____

_____

Psychomotor slowing _____

_____

Fluid intelligence _____

_____

Crystallized intelligence _____

_____

Dementia _____

_____

Alzheimer's disease _____

_____

## FILL-IN EXERCISES

Fill in the word or words that best fit in the spaces below.

1.    Studies of children who have experienced extreme deprivation during their early years provide evidence for _____ periods in humans.

2.    Some psychologists view development as occurring in stages, where behavior at one stage is _____ different from behavior at another stage.

3.    The _____ period begins at about the ninth week of prenatal development.

4.    _____ are environmental agents that can harm a developing fetus or embryo.

5.    The first two weeks after conception are referred to as the _____ period.

6.    When touched on its cheek, an infant turns its head and opens its mouth to suck. This pattern of behavior is referred to as the _____ _____.

7.    The development of motor skills in infants proceeds from _____ to _____.

8.    *Early* onset of puberty tends to be _____ *(more/less)* stressful for boys than for girls.

9.    For women the most dramatic physical change of middle adulthood is _____.

10.   The visual acuity of the newborn is estimated to be approximately _____, but improves to approximately _____ by six months.

11.   The preoperational stage is characterized by the emergence of _____ thought.

12.   In the _____ operational stage children are capable of mentally manipulating abstract as well as concrete objects, events, and ideas.

13.   In contrast to Piaget's theory which focuses on changes occurring in stages, the information-processing perspective focuses on changes that are _____.

14.   Compared to adults, children's _____ _____ (their accumulated knowledge in long-term storage) is limited because of their relative inexperience with life.

15.   Theorists who attempt to integrate Piaget's theory with information-processing views are sometimes referred to as _____-Piagetian theorists.

16. _____ _____ is a progressive and incurable illness, that occurs later in life, and causes severe impairment of memory, reasoning, language, and behavior.

## APPLICATION

### Situation

Mickey and his older brother Dave are having lunch. When their mother gives them their juice, Mickey's glass is short and fat, while Dave's is tall and thin. Although their mother is careful to pour the same amount of juice into each glass, Mickey complains that Dave got more. Their mother gets a short, fat glass from the cupboard and, while Mickey watches, pours Dave's juice from the tall, thin glass into the new short, fat one. Mickey says "That's better, now they're the same." After watching his mother pour the juice from one glass into the other, Dave just sits there chuckling. He whispers to his mother, "Boy, did you ever fool Mickey! It's the same amount of juice in both glasses!"

### Questions to answer

1. Which of Piaget's stages of cognitive development most likely describes Mickey? How about Dave?

2. What does Dave realize that Mickey doesn't? What is this concept called?

3. According to Piaget's theory, what is it that causes Mickey to think there is more juice in the second glass? What is this process called?

## USING WHAT YOU HAVE LEARNED

The chapter discusses the phenomenon of *ageism*, a prejudice against old people. It describes how subjects in a priming experiment more readily associated negative traits with the word "old" and positive traits with the word "young." These findings could reflect the stereotypes people apply to the elderly. Stereotypical beliefs about old people are actually relatively common. To get an idea of these beliefs, ask several of your friends what "old" people are like and how they differ from young people.

1. What seem to be the most common stereotypical beliefs?

2. Is there an age difference in beliefs? Do older people have the same beliefs as younger people? If they do, could these actually be a self-fulfilling prophecy?

3.    Are any of these beliefs based on fact? Compare people's beliefs with what you have read about aging in this chapter. How accurate are people's beliefs?

4.    Does providing objective information about aging alter people's beliefs. A good way to answer this would be to consider your own beliefs *before* and *after* reading Chapter 13. Did they change?


## PART THREE:    TEST AND KNOW
## SAMPLE TEST QUESTIONS

Test how well you have learned this chapter's material by answering the sample test questions. You may wish to mark your answers on a separate sheet of paper so you can reuse this test for exam review. Once you have completed the exam, check your answers and then go back to your notes and the textbook to review questions you found difficult.

1.    When considering the roles of nature and nurture, the question asked by developmental psychologists is

    a.    *Which* is more important in development-- nature or nurture?
    b.    *How much* does each contribute to development?
    c.    *How* do nature and nurture contribute to development?
    d.    all of the above

2.    Relatively discrete steps in development, through which everyone passes in the same sequence, are referred to as

    a.    sensitive periods        b.    critical periods
    c.    cohorts                d.    stages

3.    A research design used by developmental psychologists, which follows multiple cohorts longitudinally, is referred to as a

    a.    sequential study        b.    cross-sectional study
    c.    longitudinal study      d.    cohort study

4.    By about _____ weeks, the fetus is capable of sustaining life on its own.

    a.    16                 b.    22
    c.    28                 d.    32

5.   The period of greatest susceptibility to the effects of teratogens is the _____ period.

a.    gestation
b.    embryonic
c.    fetal
d.    germinal

6.   Deformed limbs, faces, ears, and genitals, as well as learning disabilities, behavior problems, and attention difficulties are associated with prenatal exposure to

a.    alcohol
b.    iron
c.    crack cocaine
d.    nicotine

7.   Which of the following does NOT decrease in older adults?

a.    crystallized intelligence
b.    ability to hear high-frequencies
c.    sexual interest
d.    visual sensitivity to contrasts

8.   Which of the following responses have been used to assess infant perception?

a.    rooting reflex; sucking
b.    orienting reflex; fixation time
c.    equilibration; disequilibration
d.    assimilation; accommodation

9.   For Piaget, the driving force behind cognitive development is

a.    assimilation
b.    accommodation
c.    equilibration
d.    operations

10.  Piaget referred to the process of modifying schemas to fit reality as

a.    adaptation
b.    accommodation
c.    assimilation
d.    equilibration

11.    A major achievement of the sensorimotor stage is the development of

a.    centration                          b.    conservation
c.    transitivity                        d.    object permanence

12.    Little Stacey loves playing peek-a-boo. Her favorite part is to cover her eyes with her hands and then call out "Nobody can see me!". Stacey is likely in which of Piaget's stages of cognitive development?

a.    formal operational                  b.    preoperational
c.    sensorimotor                        d.    concrete operational

13.    "If Louise is older than Carol, and Carol is older than Christine, which girl is the youngest?" This type of question requires an understanding of

a.    centration                          b.    conservation
c.    egocentrism                         d.    transitivity

14.    Which of the following is NOT a criticism of Piaget's theory?

a.    He paid too much attention to the type of thinking most evident in scientific or philosophical pursuits.
b.    He assumed that as children progress through the stages of cognitive development, they apply the same underlying logic in most of the things they do.
c.    He overestimated the capacities of infants and preschool children.
d.    He underestimated the role of culture in development.

15.    Children's understanding of the way they perform cognitive tasks, such as remembering, learning, and solving problems, is referred to as

a.    metacognition
b.    cognitive strategies
c.    knowledge base
d.    automatic processing

16.    According to Case, the factor most responsible for qualitative changes in cognitive development is an increasing

a.    capacity for abstract thinking
b.    ability to make use of metamemory
c.    capacity for working memory
d.    ability to perform operations

17.    The problem older people have with long-term memory appears to be

   a.    implicit memory
   b.    retrieval
   c.    storage
   d.    recognition memory

18.    Fluid intelligence

   a.    peaks in young adulthood, then levels off, and begins declining by mid adulthood
   b.    increases throughout most of life, showing declines in very old age
   c.    begins declining shortly after the preschool period, although the decline is imperceptibly slow at first
   d.    peaks at puberty, then begins a decline that accelerates with age

19.    One of the clearest changes that accompanies aging is

   a.    a decline in crystallized intelligence
   b.    a decline in abstract reasoning abilities
   c.    an erosion of the knowledge base
   d.    psychomotor slowing

20.    Alzheimer's patients have abnormally low levels of _____, a neurotransmitter that plays a central role in memory functioning.

   a.    acetylcholine
   b.    serotonin
   c.    norepinephrine
   d.    GABA

# ANSWERS

## FILL-IN EXERCISES

1. critical   2. qualitatively   3. fetal   4. teratogens   5. germinal   6. rooting reflex
7. head, toe   8. less   9. menopause   10. 20/500; 20/100   11. symbolic   12. formal
13. continuous (or quantitative)   14. knowledge base   15. neo   16. Alzheimer's disease

## APPLICATION

1.      Mickey is preoperational. Dave is concrete or formal operational.

2.      Dave realizes that the amount of juice in the glass has remained the same, even though the size and shape of the glass have changed. In other words, the basic properties of an object remain stable even though its superficial properties may be changed. This is referred to as *conservation*

3.      Mickey focuses only on one aspect of the glass -- its height, and ignores the difference between the two glasses in width. *Centration*

## SAMPLE TEST QUESTIONS

| | | | | |
|---|---|---|---|---|
| 1. | c | | 11. | d |
| 2. | d | | 12. | b |
| 3. | a | | 13. | d |
| 4. | c | | 14. | c |
| 5. | b | | 15. | a |
| 6. | a | | 16. | c |
| 7. | a | | 17. | b |
| 8. | b | | 18. | a |
| 9. | c | | 19. | d |
| 10. | b | | 20. | a |

# Chapter 14
# SOCIAL DEVELOPMENT

## PART ONE:   PRE-READ AND WORK
## OUTLINE AND LEARNING OBJECTIVES

Pre-read this chapter's table of contents and end-of-chapter summary. Then, use the outline segment-by-segment to help you work through the chapter. Jot down your own questions, comments, and notes in the space provided. Make a note of key terms and of difficult areas that you will need to review (include page numbers). Then, answer the questions in the learning objectives section that follows. Check off those you are confident that you can answer well. Re-read the material in the text for the questions about which you are less confident. Record the important points from your reading in the space below each question.

## OUTLINE

I.   ATTACHMENT

  A. Attachment in Infancy

  B. Individual Differences in Attachment Patterns

  C. **From Mind to Brain:** Temperament and Experience in Attachment Style

  D. Implications of Attachment for Later Development

II.   SOCIALIZATION

A. The Role of Parents

B. The Role of Culture

C. **A Global Vista:** Parental Acceptance and Rejection in Cross-Cultural
Perspective

D. Socialization of Gender

III.   PEER RELATIONSHIPS

A. Friendships

B. Sibling Relationships

IV.   DEVELOPMENT OF SOCIAL COGNITION

A. The Evolving Self-Concept

B. Concepts of Others

C. Perspective-Taking and Theory of Mind

D. Children's Understanding of Gender

## V.  Moral Development

### A. The Role of Cognition

### B. The Role of Emotion

### C. **Commentary**: Making Sense of Moral Development

## VI.  Social Development Across the Lifespan

### A. Childhood

### B. Adolescence

### C. Early Adulthood

D. Middle Age

E. Old Age

## VII.  SOME CONCLUDING THOUGHTS

## LEARNING OBJECTIVES

Upon completion of Chapter 14, you should be able to answer the following questions.

1.    Describe the emergence of attachment behavior in infancy.

2.    What is imprinting and how is it similar to attachment?

3.    How does the Strange Situation behavior of securely attached infants differ from that of infants who are anxious-avoidant, anxious-ambivalent, and disorganized?

4.    How is attachment possibly related to temperament?

5.    How can mother's sensitivity to her infant's signals affect attachment?

6.    How does the later adjustment of securely attached infants differ from that of insecurely attached infants?

7.    What is meant by adult attachment style? How is the attachment style of parents related to that of their infants?

8.    What are the positive and negative effects of day care on attachment? What factors may contribute to these effects?

9.    What are the characteristics and effects of each of the three styles of parenting identified by Diana Baumrind?

10.    Discuss how parental acceptance and rejection may differ across cultures, yet be similar in their effects.

11.    What role do adults play in the socialization of gender roles?

12.    What changes take place across age in the meaning of friendship to children and in the roles that friends play?

13.    How do rejected children differ from neglected children in terms of both their behavior and how their peers respond to them?

14.    What are the characteristics of sibling relationships?

15.    How do children's descriptions of themselves and others change across age?.

16.    How is the development of theory of mind related to perspective taking?

17.    What changes occur across age in children's perspective taking?

18.    Compare between the following three stages of children's understanding of gender: gender identity, gender stability, gender constancy.

19.    What are gender schemas?

20.    Discuss the biological/evolutionary and cultural/social-learning explanations for gender differences in aggression and nurturance.

21.    According to the social-cognitive view, how is prosocial behavior acquired?

22.    How do Piaget's stages of morality of constraint and morality of cooperation differ?

23.    What are Kohlberg's three levels of moral reasoning? Provide examples of answers to the Heinz dilemma for each level.

24.    Outline the sequence of judgments that comprise the information-processing model of moral decision making.

25.    Explain the psychoanalytic view of moral development.

26.    How does empathy develop in children?

27.    What are the advantages and shortcomings associated with the cognitive and emotional approaches to moral development?

28.    What is the major crisis or developmental task of each of Erikson's eight stages of psychosocial development?

29.    For each of Erikson's psychosocial stages, what are the corresponding stages, if applicable, from both Freud's and Piaget's theories?

30.    How do the conflict and continuity models differ in their view of adolescence?

## PART TWO:    REVIEW AND LEARN
## KEY TERMS, FILL-IN EXERCISES, APPLICATION AND USING WHAT YOU HAVE LEARNED

Before doing the exercises below, review the information you learned in this chapter. Reread the work you did in part one of this study guide chapter, plus the interim summaries and end-of-chapter summary in your textbook. Review any problem areas. Once you feel comfortable with the material, do the following exercises without referring to your notes or textbook. If you have difficulty with a term or question, mark it and come back to it. When you have finished an exercise, go back to your notes and the textbook to find the answers to the questions that gave you difficulty. Finally, check your answers (key terms against the textbook and the rest against the answer key).

## KEY TERMS

Attachment _____

_____

Imprinting _____

_____

Separation anxiety _____

_____

Strange Situation _____

_____

Securely attached _____

_____

Avoidant style _____

_____

Ambivalent style _____

_____

Disorganized style _____

_____

Internal working model _____

_____

Adult attachment _____

_____

Socialization _____

_____

Authoritarian parents _____

_____

Permissive parents _____

_____

Authoritative parents _____

_____

Gender roles _____

_____

Gender _____

_____

Sex typing _____

_____

Rejected children _____

_____

Neglected children _____

_____

Social cognition _____

_____

Self-concept _____

_____

Perspective-taking _____

_____

Theory of mind _____

_____

Gender identity _____

_____

Gender stability _____

_____

Gender constancy _____

_____

Gender schemas _____

_____

Sex-role ideology _____

_____

Androgenital syndrome (AGS) _____

_____

Morality _____

_____

Morality of constraint _____

_____

Morality of cooperation _____

_____

Preconventional morality _____

_____

Conventional morality _____

_____

Postconventional morality _____

_____

Prosocial behavior _____

_____

Empathy _____

_____

Empathic distress _____

_____

Psychosocial stages _____

_____

Developmental task_____

_____

Basic trust versus mistrust _____

_____

Autonomy versus shame and doubt _____

_____

Initiative versus guilt _____

_____

Industry versus inferiority _____

_____

Identity versus identity confusion _____

_____

Initiation rites _____

_____

Negative identity    _____

_____

Conflict model    _____

_____

Continuity model    _____

_____

Intimacy versus isolation    _____

_____

Generativity versus stagnation    _____

_____

Integrity versus despair    _____

_____

## FILL-IN EXERCISES

Fill in the word or words that best fit in the spaces below.

1.   The attachment figure serves as a safe _____ from which the child can explore the environment.

2.   Babies visually recognize their mother at about _____ months of age and, by about _____ or _____ months, recognize and greet their mothers and other attachment figures from across the room.

3.   Cross-cultural research, as well as research with blind infants, suggests that separation anxiety is _____ based.

4.   In the Strange Situation, infants who welcome their mother after her absence and seek closeness with her are described as _____ attached.

5.   Bowlby proposed that an infant develops a(n) _____ _____ model of the attachment relationship that forms the basis for expectations in other close relationships.

6. _____ involves learning the rules, beliefs, values, skills, attitudes, and behavior patterns of society.

7. Parents who place a high value on obedience and respect for authority are described as _____ parents; those who impose virtually no controls on their children are referred to as _____ parents; while those who set and enforce standards, but also encourage verbal give and take are called _____ parents.

8. While a person's sex is based on genetic and anatomical differences, his or her gender is influenced by _____.

9. Friendships in children begin to emerge around the _____ year of life.

10. Adolescents are more concerned than younger children with _____ in friendships.

11. Children who are rarely picked by their classmates as either someone they really like or someone they really dislike are referred to as _____ children.

12. Children's understanding of themselves, others, and relationships is referred to as _____ _____.

13. _____ _____ refers to the ability to understand other people's viewpoints.

14. The ability to correctly label oneself as either a boy or a girl is called _____ _____ and usually emerges by about _____ years of age.

15. The term _____ refers to the set of rules people use for balancing the conflicting interests of themselves and others.

16. Viewing rules as unchanging and immutable is one of the characteristics of the stage Piaget called the morality of _____.

17. According to Kohlberg's theory, the desire to gain the approval or avoid the disapproval of others characterizes the level of _____ morality.

18. According to the _____ model, moral reasoning involves making a series of sequential judgments about whether an act is immoral and whether it deserves punishment.

19. The psychodynamic view of moral development proposes that children start out relatively _____, or self-centered and interested in gratifying their own needs.

20. According to the psychodynamic view, children take the values of their parents and gradually _____ them by adopting them as their own.

21.    Discrepancies between what people feel they should do and what they observe themselves doing result in _____.

22.    Erikson's model is comprised of eight _____ stages of development.

23.    Some adolescents adopt a _____ _____, taking on a role that society defines as bad, but which provides them with a sense that at least they are something.

## APPLICATION

In Chapter 14, you learned about the challenges or developmental tasks faced by individuals at different stages in their lives, according to Erikson's theory. Each of the descriptions that follow translates one of Erikson's developmental tasks into a conflict faced by a particular individual. For each description, match the psychosocial stage that corresponds to the challenge they're facing. (Note: Some stages appear more than once.)

**Psychosocial Stages**

Basic Trust versus Mistrust
Autonomy versus Shame and Doubt
Initiative versus Guilt
Industry versus Inferiority

Identity versus Identity Confusion
Intimacy versus Isolation
Generativity versus Stagnation
Integrity versus Despair

**Conflicts**

1.    Paul is a "professional student." He has studied engineering, general arts, history, psychology, and criminology. Now, he feels maybe he should leave university and try business for a while.

2.    Monica spends a lot of time playing make-believe. She really enjoys dressing up in different adult costumes, pretending to be the role she dresses as. She loves dreaming up ideas and carrying them out.

3.    Ronny loves sports at school. He's quite athletic and is always trying to show that he's better than anyone else on the soccer team.

4.    Since her kids left home, Diane has been toying with the idea of becoming a scout leader. She thought she'd like all the time she'd have to herself when the kids grew up, but, in fact, she finds her life feels really empty with them gone.

5.    Sarah hangs out with a group of skin heads. They hang around the shopping plaza doing nothing and seem to delight in offending some of the shoppers by their foul language and appearance.

6.    Ian has been avoiding Jennifer. He likes her and she likes him. But, he's afraid to get too close. Their relationship is starting to get serious and that scares Ian.

7.  Geoff has been having problems with reading at school. Compared to other kids he's far behind. It's especially hard when they take turns reading aloud. He slouches down in his desk and tries to hide so that the teacher won't call on him.

8.  Guy has run a successful TV repair business for 20 years. Last year he sold the business to spend his time teaching TV repair to physically disabled teenagers.

9.  Sonia is always trying to do things on her own. She seems proud of the fact that she can now stand on her own two feet. In fact, she often insists on doing things like feeding herself, even if it means getting the food all over herself.

## USING WHAT YOU HAVE LEARNED

A group of students has just covered social development in their Introduction to Psychology course. The topic of attachment in infancy was particularly interesting, and a topic they hadn't given much thought to, previously. The students get into a discussion concerning whether attachment is important and what role a mother plays in her infant's attachment. Your job is to decide whether each student's opinion is accurate or not, based on your readings in the text.

*Student #1:* "As far as I'm concerned, attachment isn't very important. Sure you can't just ignore babies; you have to feed them and change them. But all this 'lovey-dovey' stuff just makes their parents feel good. It's not important for the baby. How babies feel about their mothers isn't important in the long run."

*Student #2:* "Well, I think attachment is VERY important! Once a baby has formed an insecure attachment, there isn't very much you can do to change things. They'll be messed up for life!"

*Student #3:* "I've been thinking about what causes insecure attachment and it's got to be the mother's fault. Mothers are totally to blame if their baby is insecurely attached. It has to do with how they treat their baby, and that's all there is to it."

*Student #4:* "I think there's too much 'mother-bashing' that goes on when people talk about attachment. Everybody says it's the mother's fault. So if a baby isn't securely attached, who gets blamed? The mother! What a load of guilt to put on someone. What about the baby? Are babies all the same? Aren't some babies more easily scared than others, no matter what their mother does?"

*Student #5:* "Well, if attachment is important, then I've got real concerns about day care. It can't be good for your new baby. Aren't psychologists concerned about the effects of daycare?"

## PART THREE:   TEST AND KNOW
## SAMPLE TEST QUESTIONS

Test how well you have learned this chapter's material by answering the sample test questions.  You may wish to mark your answers on a separate sheet of paper so you can reuse this test for exam review.  Once you have completed the exam, check your answers and then go back to your notes and the textbook to review questions you found difficult.

1.    Separation anxiety emerges at about the same time as

   a.    the infant is able to stand alone
   b.    the infant begins to walk
   c.    the infant is weaned
   d.    the infant begins to crawl

2.    Sally was very upset when her mother left her alone in the Strange Situation. When her mother returned, Sally was angry at her, yet at the same time sought to be close to her. Sally's attachment pattern is best described as

   a.    disorganized
   b.    securely attached
   c.    ambivalent
   d.    avoidant

3.    Infants who are securely attached are more likely than those who are insecurely attached to have mothers who

   a.    are responsive to their communications
   b.    are psychologically accessible
   c.    convey a sense of acceptance and enjoyment
   d.    all of the above

4.    Adults who dismiss the importance of attachment relationships or offer idealized generalizations about their parents which they are unable to back up with specific examples tend to display a(n) _____ adult attachment style.

   a.    secure
   b.    ambivalent
   c.    avoidant
   d.    unresolved/disorganized

5. Parents who place high value on obedience and respect for authority and do not encourage discussion of *why* particular behaviors are important are described as

   a. authoritarian
   b. permissive
   c. authoritative
   d. disorganized

6. Low self-reliance and poor control over aggressive impulses is associated with which parenting style?

   a. authoritarian
   b. permissive
   c. authoritative
   d. disorganized

7. Parents often treat their sons and daughters differently from an early age. Girls in Europe and North America, in contrast to boys receive more

   a. punishment.
   b. encouragement to compete.
   c. warmth and affection.
   d. pressure not to cry.

8. Neglected children tend to be

   a. ignored by their peers
   b. disliked by their peers
   c. hostile and aggressive
   d. at risk for later delinquency

9. When asked to describe himself, Sid replies "I'm good at math, and I'm the best skateboarder in my school." Based on his description, Sid is likely around

   a. 3 years of age
   b. 6 years of age
   c. 10 years of age
   d. 17 years of age

10. In the game "Decoy and Defender" a child simply moves her flag carrier as quickly as possible across the board, totally failing to take into account her opponent's perspective. Such an egocentric strategy would be typical of a(n)

   a. 1 to 2 year old
   b. 3 to 6 year old
   c. 6 to 8 year old
   d. 8 to 10 year old

11.     Gender constancy refers to children's

    a.     tendency to play and form friendships primarily with same-sex peers
    b.     realization that their gender remains constant over time
    c.     ability to categorize themselves and others according to gender
    d.     realization that a person's gender cannot be altered by changes in appearance or activities

12.     Mental representations that associate psychological characteristics with one sex or the other are referred to as

    a.     gender schemas        b.     gender roles
    c.     sex typing           d.     gender constancy

13.     The majority of preindustrial societies socialize boys from an early age to be

    a.     self-reliant         b.     self-restrained
    c.     responsible         d.     obedient

14.     When one child tries to change the rules to a game of marbles, the child she is playing with gets very upset, shouting "You're not allowed to break the rules!" The second child is likely at which level of moral development?

    a.     morality of cooperation
    b.     postconventional morality
    c.     morality of constraint
    d.     conventional morality

15.     After listening to the Heinz dilemma, an individual responds that Heinz should steal the drug, because the law is never more important than a human life. This answer is characteristic of which of Kohlberg's levels of moral development?

    a.     morality of cooperation
    b.     postconventional morality
    c.     morality of constraint
    d.     conventional morality

16.     According to cognitive-social theories of moral development, children learn that certain acts are wrong and will be punished because they

    a.     are punished for the act
    b.     see someone else punished
    c.     are told they will be punished
    d.     all of the above

17. When 13-month-old Fred saw his mother crying, he offered her his soother as a way of trying to comfort her. Fred's behavior was likely motivated by the feeling of

   a.    empathic distress
   b.    guilt
   c.    narcissism
   d.    morality

18. Kohlberg's theory of moral development has been criticized as biased against women because

   a.    Kohlberg never examined the moral reasoning of women in his research
   b.    women's moral concerns are more likely to center on issues of care and responsibility, rather than duty, law, and order
   c.    women's moral concerns are more likely to center on issues of duty, law, and order, rather than care and responsibility
   d.    men are very concerned with obeying the rules, whereas women are not

19. Erikson's psychosocial stage that corresponds to Freud's anal stage is

   a.    initiative vs. guilt
   b.    trust vs. mistrust
   c.    industry vs. inferiority
   d.    autonomy vs. shame and doubt

20. According to Erikson, _____ occurs when an individual fails to develop a coherent and enduring sense of self, and has difficulty committing to roles, values, people, and occupational choices.

   a.    the midlife crisis
   b.    despair
   c.    identity confusion
   d.    stagnation

# ANSWERS

## FILL-IN EXERCISES

1. base   2. three; five, six   3. maturationally   4. securely   5. internal working
6. socialization   7. authoritarian; permissive; authoritative   8. learning   9. third
10. intimacy   11. neglected   12. social cognition   13. perspective taking   14. gender
identity; two   15. morality   16. constraint   17. conventional   18. information-processing
19. narcissistic   20. internalize   21. guilt   22. psychosocial   23. negative identity

## APPLICATION

1. identity versus identity diffusion   2. initiative versus guilt   3. industry versus
inferiority   4. generativity versus stagnation   5. identity versus identity diffusion
6. intimacy versus isolation   7. industry versus inferiority   8. generativity versus
stagnation   9. autonomy versus shame and doubt

## USING WHAT YOU HAVE LEARNED

1. No. Attachment is important. It is related to later social and academic competence,
and may be influential throughout life, perhaps influencing adult attachment.
2. No. While disturbed attachment does predict later adjustment problems, this is not
always the case, nor is attachment style unchangeable.
3. No. While maternal responsiveness is very important, it is not the only variable to
affect attachment. Temperament and environmental factors also are important.
4. Yes. Temperament may be very important. The three infant temperaments – easy,
difficult, and slow-to-warm-up – may correspond to secure, ambivalent, and avoidant
attachment styles. Inborn timidity may also be related.
 5. Yes. Psychologists are concerned about the possible effects of daycare on attachment.
Results are not that clear.

## SAMPLE TEST QUESTIONS

| | | | |
|---|---|---|---|
| 1. | d | 11. | d |
| 2. | c | 12. | a |
| 3. | d | 13. | a |
| 4. | c | 14. | c |
| 5. | a | 15. | b |
| 6. | b | 16. | d |
| 7. | c | 17. | a |
| 8. | a | 18. | b |
| 9. | c | 19. | d |
| 10. | b | 20. | c |

# Chapter 15
# PSYCHOLOGICAL DISORDERS

## PART ONE: PRE-READ AND WORK
## OUTLINE AND LEARNING OBJECTIVES

Pre-read this chapter's table of contents and end-of-chapter summary. Then, use the outline segment-by-segment to help you work through the chapter. Jot down your own questions, comments, and notes in the space provided. Make a note of key terms and of difficult areas that you will need to review (include page numbers). Then, answer the questions in the learning objectives section that follows. Check off those you are confident that you can answer well. Re-read the material in the text for the questions about which you are less confident. Record the important points from your reading in the space below each question.

## OUTLINE

I. THE CULTURAL CONTEXT OF PSYCHOPATHOLOGY

    A. Culture and Psychopathology

    B. Is Mental Illness Nothing but a Cultural Construction?

II. CONTEMPORARY APPROACHES TO PSYCHOPATHOLOGY

    A. Psychodynamic Perspective

    B. Cognitive-Behavioral Perspective

C. Biological Approach

D. Systems Approach

E. Evolutionary Perspective

III.   DESCRIPTIVE DIAGNOSES: DSM-IV AND PSYCHOLOGICAL
       SYNDROMES

A. DSM-IV

B. Disorders Usually First Diagnosed in Infancy, Childhood, or Adolescence

C. Substance-Related Disorders

D. Schizophrenia

E. Mood Disorders

F. **A Global Vista:** Depression on a Hopi Reservation

## LEARNING OBJECTIVES

Upon completion of Chapter 15, you should be able to answer the following questions.

1.    How is psychopathology influenced by culture?

2.    What is labeling theory? How did the research Rosenhan conducted in mental institutions support this view of psychopathology?

3.    What criticisms have been voiced concerning both the "mental illness is a myth" and labeling theory approaches?

4.    What are the differences between neuroses, personality disorders, and psychoses?

5.    What are the three questions that comprise a psychodynamic formulation?

6.    How do the behavioral and cognitive approaches conceptualize psychopathology?

7.    How does the biological approach conceptualize mental disorders?

8.    How do psychologists with a family systems approach view psychopathology?

9.    How would psychopathology be explained by evolutionary psychologists?

10. What are the five axes that make up DSM-IV's multiaxial system of diagnosis?

11. What are the similarities and differences between attention-deficit hyperactivity disorder (ADHD) and conduct disorder?

12. How do both genetic and environmental factors account for the findings that alcoholism runs in families?

13. What are the major characteristics of schizophrenia?

14. What are the differences between paranoid, catatonic, and disorganized schizophrenia?

15. How does the dopamine hypothesis account for both the positive and negative symptoms of schizophrenia?

16. Discuss the evidence indicating that both biological and environmental factors contribute to schizophrenia.

17. What are the differences between major depressive disorder, dysthymic disorder, and bipolar depressive disorder?

18. Discuss the contributions of genetic factors, neurotransmitters, and environmental factors to depression.

19. What are the four types of cognitive distortions in depressive thinking described by Beck? Provide examples for each.

20.    How does the psychodynamic view of depression differ from the cognitive view?

21.    How does culture influence the way people view and experience depression?

22.    Describe the symptoms of the following anxiety disorders:

Phobia

Panic disorder

Agoraphobia

Obsessive-compulsive disorder

Posttraumatic stress disorder (PTSD)

23.    How do genetic vulnerability, environmental factors, and stress contribute to anxiety?

24.    Describe the classical conditioning and cognitive explanations of anxiety reactions.

25.    How does Barlow's model integrate avoidance learning and autonomic arousal to explain the development of panic attacks?

26.    Compare and contrast the psychodynamic and cognitive-behavioral views of anxiety.

27.    What are the symptoms of dissociative disorders? How is childhood trauma related to the development of these disorders?

28.   What are the symptoms of borderline personality disorder and antisocial personality disorder? What similarities and differences are there in the etiology of each disorder?

29.   How can politics influence the classification of psychiatric disorders?

## PART TWO:    REVIEW AND LEARN
## KEY TERMS, FILL-IN EXERCISES, APPLICATION AND USING WHAT YOU HAVE LEARNED

Before doing the exercises below, review the information you learned in this chapter. Reread the work you did in part one of this study guide chapter, plus the interim summaries and end-of-chapter summary in your textbook. Review any problem areas. Once you feel comfortable with the material, do the following exercises without referring to your notes or textbook. If you have difficulty with a term or question, mark it and come back to it. When you have finished an exercise, go back to your notes and the textbook to find the answers to the questions that gave you difficulty. Finally, check your answers (key terms against the textbook and the rest against the answer key).

## KEY TERMS

Psychopathology    _____

_____

Labeling theory    _____

_____

Neuroses    _____

_____

Personality disorders    _____

_____

Psychoses    _____

_____

Psychodynamic formulation    _____

_____

Cognitive-behavioral    _____

_____

Mental status_____

_____

Diathesis-stress model    _____

_____

Systems approach    _____

_____

Family systems model    _____

_____

Family homeostatic mechanisms    _____

_____

Family roles _____

_____

Boundaries    _____

_____

Family alliances    _____

_____

Diagnostic and Statistical Manual of Mental Disorders (DSM-IV)  _____

_____

Descriptive diagnosis        _____

_____

Clinical syndrome    _____

_____

Medical model        _____

_____

Multiaxial system of diagnosis    _____

_____

Attention-deficit hyperactivity disorder (ADHD)    _____

_____

Conduct disorder        _____

_____

Substance-related disorders        _____

_____

Alcoholism    _____

_____

Schizophrenia        _____

_____

Delusion        _____

_____

Hallucination _____

_____

Loosening of associations _____

_____

Negative symptoms _____

_____

Positive symptoms _____

_____

Paranoid schizophrenia _____

_____

Catatonic schizophrenia _____

_____

Disorganized schizophrenia _____

_____

Dopamine hypothesis _____

_____

Family roles _____

_____

Ventricles _____

_____

Mood disorders _____

_____

Major depressive disorder _____

_____

Anhedonia _____

_____

Dysthymic disorder _____

_____

Bipolar disorder _____

_____

Mania _____

_____

Unipolar depression _____

_____

Negative triad _____

_____

Cognitive Distortions _____

_____

Anxiety disorders _____

_____

Generalized anxiety disorder _____

_____

Phobia _____

_____

Panic disorder _____

_____

Agoraphobia _____

_____

Obsessive-compulsive disorder _____

_____

Obsession _____

_____

Compulsion _____

_____

Posttraumatic stress disorder (PTSD) _____

_____

Dissociative disorders _____

_____

Dissociation _____

_____

Dissociative identity disorder _____

_____

Personality disorders _____

_____

Narcissistic personality disorder _____

_____

Borderline personality disorder  _____

_____

Antisocial personality disorder  _____

_____

Schizoaffective disorder  _____

_____

Seasonal affective disorder (SAD)_____

_____

## FILL-IN EXERCISES

Fill in the word or words that best fit in the spaces below.

1.  Thomas Szasz argued that mental illness is a _____.

2.  Clinicians who adhere to a cognitive perspective focus on the patient's irrational _____ that maintain dysfunctional behaviors and emotions.

3.  The _____-_____ model holds that people with an underlying vulnerability may exhibit symptoms under stressful circumstances.

4.  Systems theorists refer to the methods family members use to preserve equilibrium in a family as family _____ mechanisms.

5.  Family _____ are parts individuals play in repetitive family dramas, according to system theorists.

6.  In descriptive diagnosis, constellations of symptoms that tend to occur together are referred to as clinical _____.

7.  Attention-deficit hyperactivity disorder is characterized by _____, _____, and hyperactivity.

8.  Attention-deficit hyperactivity disorder is more prevalent in _____ (males/females) than in _____ (males/females) .

9.   As in other Western countries, the third largest health problem in the United States today, following heart disease and cancer, is _____.

10.  Delusions of persecution are characteristic of _____ _____.

11.  Extended periods of frozen movement and stupor are characteristic of _____ _____.

12.  _____ describes a loss of interest in pleasurable activities, characteristic of major depressive disorder.

13.  Individuals with _____ disorder tend to achieve high levels of education and are disproportionately represented among creative writers and other professionals.

14.  According to Beck, cognitive distortions involve a depressed person's transforming neutral or positive information in a _____ direction.

15.  From a _____ perspective, depression cannot be isolated from the personality structure of the person experiencing it.

16.  _____ are persistent thoughts or ideas that cause distress and interfere with an individual's life.

17.  According to David Barlow, as autonomic responses such as quickened pulse, pounding heart, and difficulty breathing become associated with the panic state through classical conditioning, people with panic disorders often develop a fear of _____.

## APPLICATION

Identify the disorder that best describes the following fictitious examples.

1.   An 8-year-old boy is having troubles in school. He cannot sit still at his desk, has trouble focusing on class work, and impulsively calls out answers without putting his hand up. He's been getting into arguments and fights lately with other kids, although his teacher thinks it may be due to his negative feelings about school.

2.   A writer has periods where she produces so much work that her friends are amazed. She's on an emotional high during her productive periods, and can get by with only a couple of hours of sleep each day. But she has other periods when she can't seem to write anything; she can't concentrate; in fact, she often can't even get out of bed for days at a time. During these times, nothing interests her, even things she usually loves to do.

3.  A restaurant worker has a persistent fear that he has inadvertently contaminated the food he is preparing with a poisonous compound. He repeatedly throws out the food and starts from scratch, meticulously writing down every ingredient he adds to the meal.

4.  An individual is afraid to leave her house and travel to work because of a fear of experiencing a panic attack on the subway or at the office.

5.  A 25-year-old gets into trouble with the law repeatedly for stealing and destroying the property of innocent victims. When caught, he shows no remorse and no concern for the harm he has caused his victims. He is extremely charming, however, and easily finds new victims to con.

6.  A young man is convinced that the government is out to frame him and ruin his business. He suspects everyone who comes into his office of being a government agent. Furthermore, he is convinced that the FBI has bugged his office and may actually be attempting to read his thoughts using microwaves.

## USING WHAT YOU HAVE LEARNED

Beck's approach to depression emphasizes cognitive errors in the reasoning of depressed individuals. Below are some hypothetical situations involving such errors. Provide the most appropriate label for each error.

1.  A stranger approaching an individual on the sidewalk suddenly crosses the street and begins walking on the other side. The individual concludes "He thinks I'm awful and can't stand to pass near me."

2.  After being turned down for one date, a depressed man concludes, "I'm unattractive to women and I'll never get a date."

3.  Ignoring her grade of A- on the midterm exam, a student asked, "Why can't I do well in this course?"

4.  After being pulled over for going 10 mph over the limit, a driver concludes "This is terrible, I'm going to lose my license!" When informed by the police that all he was getting was a warning ticket, he concluded "It's just as bad, they 'll never let me renew my insurance after this!"

5.  After three years of repair-free driving, George's car got a flat tire when he drove over a broken bottle. He says to his friend, "I should never have bought this stupid car. It's nothing but a lemon!"

## PART THREE:    TEST AND KNOW
## SAMPLE TEST QUESTIONS

Test how well you have learned this chapter's material by answering the sample test questions.  You may wish to mark your answers on a separate sheet of paper so you can reuse this test for exam review.  Once you have completed the exam, check your answers and then go back to your notes and the textbook to review questions you found difficult.

1.    According to psychiatrist Thomas Szasz

   a.    mental illness is a myth
   b.    panic disorders represent a fear of fear
   c.    psychiatric illness is in the eye of the beholder
   d.    the symptoms of any individual are really indicative of disruptions in the individual's family

2.    Psychodynamic theorists distinguish among three broad classes of psychopathology

   a.    neuroses, anxiety disorders, and psychoses
   b.    affective disorders, personality disorders, and psychoses
   c.    dissociative disorders, personality disorders, and psychoses
   d.    neuroses, personality disorders and psychoses

3.    Descriptive diagnosis tends to be most compatible with

   a.    the behavioral approach to psychopathology
   b.    the medical model of psychopathology
   c.    the cognitive approach to psychopathology
   d.    the systems approach to psychopathology

4.    The prevalence of ADHD is estimated at _____ of school-aged children.

   a.    3-5%                    b.    10-12%
   c.    15-18%                  d.    20-25%

5.    Research suggests that some children with conduct disorder

   a.    are oversensitive to rewards and punishments
   b.    are subject to delusions and hallucinations
   c.    are difficult to condition
   d.    frequently display self-mutilating behavior

6. The best predictor of whether someone will develop alcoholism is

    a. the presence of an anxiety disorder
    b. a history of conduct disorder or antisocial personality disorder
    c. a family history of mood disorder
    d. a family history of alcoholism

7. DSM-IV recognizes three main subtypes of schizophrenia

    a. bipolar, catatonic, and paranoid
    b. paranoid, unipolar, and catatonic
    c. paranoid, catatonic, and seasonal
    d. catatonic, paranoid, and disorganized

8. One member of a pair of MZ twins is diagnosed with schizophrenia, while the other remains healthy. What are the chances that the offspring of the healthy twin will develop schizophrenia?

    a. slim, since the parent does not have schizophrenia
    b. about the same as the chances of anyone else in the general population
    c. impossible to determine
    d. about the same as the offspring of the twin with schizophrenia

9. Too little dopamine transmission in the circuit that projects from the midbrain to the prefrontal cortex is associated with the

    a. negative symptoms of schizophrenia
    b. mood fluctuations in seasonal affective disorder
    c. low conditionability of individuals with antisocial personality disorder
    d. false alarms associated with anxiety disorders

10. A chronic, low-level depression of more than two years' duration, interrupted by short intervals of normal moods is referred to as

    a. seasonal affective disorder
    b. dysthymic disorder
    c. bipolar depression
    d. anhedonia

11. A _____ episode refers to a period of abnormally elevated or expansive mood.

    a. catatonic             b. agoraphobic
    c. manic                d. borderline

12. The neurotransmitter that seems to be involved in schizophrenia is

    a.    dopamine
    b.    GABA
    c.    norepinephrine
    d.    acetylcholine

13. Beck describes the negative triad as a negative outlook on

    a.    the past, present, and future
    b.    the self, family, and others
    c.    the world, self, and future
    d.    working, loving, and happiness

14. Unlike cognitive theorists, who focus on faulty cognition, psychodynamic explanations of depression focus on

    a.    aggression              b.    dopamine
    c.    labeling                d.    motivation

15. Nightmares, flashbacks, hypervigilance, exaggerated startle responses, and psychological numbness are symptoms associated with

    a.    seasonal affective disorder
    b.    disorganized schizophrenia
    c.    obsessive-compulsive disorder
    d.    posttraumatic stress disorder

16. Roughly 80% of patients suffering from panic attacks

    a.    describe a stressful, negative life event that coincided with their first attack
    b.    report a history of physical or sexual abuse
    c.    attribute negative or malevolent intentions to other people and expect abuse and rejection
    d.    experience extremely unstable interpersonal relationships

17. Disruptions in consciousness, memory, sense of identity, or perceptions are characteristic of

    a.    panic attacks
    b.    narcissistic personality disorder
    c.    borderline personality disorder
    d.    dissociative disorders

18. Psychodynamic theorists argue that _____ originates in pathological attachment relationships in early childhood, which lead to attachment problems later in life.

    a. borderline personality disorder
    b. narcissistic personality disorder
    c. obsessive-compulsive disorder
    d. catatonic schizophrenia

19. In explaining the development of antisocial personality disorder, both social learning and psychodynamic approaches implicate

    a. the importance of a sexually abusive male relative
    b. physical abuse, neglect, and absent or criminal male role models
    c. the importance of both anxiety and mood disorders in the individual's family
    d. a high incidence of expressed emotion in the individual's family

20. Schizoaffective disorder refers to

    a. a depressive syndrome that occurs primarily in the winter
    b. a mixture of anxiety and depression
    c. a disorder that involves attributes of both schizophrenia and psychotic depression
    d. a disorder characterized by alternating cycles of elation and depression

# ANSWERS

## FILL-IN EXERCISES

1. myth  2. beliefs  3. diathesis-stress  4. homeostatic  5. roles  6. syndromes
7. inattention, impulsivity  8. males; females  9. alcoholism  10. paranoid schizophrenia
11. catatonic schizophrenia  12. anhedonia  13. bipolar  14. depressive  (or negative)
15. psychodynamic  16. obsessions  17. fear

## APPLICATION

1. attention-deficit hyperactivity disorder  2. bipolar disorder  3. obsessive-compulsive
disorder  4. agoraphobia  5. antisocial personality disorder  6. paranoid schizophrenia

## USING WHAT YOU HAVE LEARNED

1. personalization  2. overgeneralization  3. arbitrary inference  4. magnification
5. arbitrary inference

## SAMPLE TEST QUESTIONS

| | | | |
|---|---|---|---|
| 1. | a | 11. | c |
| 2. | d | 12. | a |
| 3. | b | 13. | c |
| 4. | a | 14. | d |
| 5. | c | 15. | d |
| 6. | d | 16. | a |
| 7. | d | 17. | d |
| 8. | d | 18. | a |
| 9. | a | 19. | b |
| 10. | b | 20. | c |

# Chapter 16
# TREATMENT OF PSYCHOLOGICAL DISORDERS

PART ONE:     PRE-READ AND WORK
OUTLINE AND LEARNING OBJECTIVES

Pre-read this chapter's table of contents and end-of-chapter summary. Then, use the outline segment-by-segment to help you work through the chapter. Jot down your own questions, comments, and notes in the space provided. Make a note of key terms and of difficult areas that you will need to review (include page numbers). Then, answer the questions in the learning objectives section that follows. Check off those you are confident that you can answer well. Re-read the material in the text for the questions about which you are less confident. Record the important points from your reading in the space below each question.

## OUTLINE

I.   PSYCHODYNAMIC THERAPIES

   A. Therapeutic Techniques

   B. Varieties of Psychodynamic Therapy

II.  COGNITIVE-BEHAVIORAL THERAPIES

   A. Basic Principles

   B. Classical Conditioning Techniques

   C. Operant Conditioning Techniques

D. Modeling

E. Skills Training

F. Cognitive Therapy

## III.  HUMANISTIC, GROUP, AND FAMILY THERAPIES

A. Humanistic Therapies

B. Group Therapies

C. Family Therapies

## IV.  BIOLOGICAL TREATMENTS

A. **From Mind to Brain:** Psychotropic Medications

B. Antipsychotic Medications

C. Antidepressant and Mood Stabilizing Medications

D. Antianxiety Medications

E. Electroconvulsive Therapy and Psychosurgery

V.  EVALUATING PSYCHOLOGICAL TREATMENTS

A. Pharmacotherapy

B. Psychotherapy

C. **Commentary:** Are All Treatments Created Equal?

D: **One Step Further:** Psychotherapy Integration

VI.  THE BROADER CONTEXT OF PSYCHOLOGICAL TREATMENT

A. **A Global Vista:** Culture and Psychotherapy

B. The Economics of Mental Health Care

## VII.   SOME CONCLUDING THOUGHTS

## LEARNING OBJECTIVES

Upon completion of Chapter 16, you should be able to answer the following questions.

1.    What are the two principles underlying the psychodynamic approach to therapeutic change?

2.    What three techniques are used by psychodynamic therapists?

3.    What are the similarities and differences between psychoanalysis and psychodynamic psychotherapy?

4.    What are the four steps involved in systematic desensitization?

5.    What are the differences between counter-conditioning and extinction as explanations of how systematic desensitization works?

6.    How does flooding differ from graded exposure?

7.    What are the principles underlying the token economy procedure?

8.  How does participatory modeling work to alleviate fear responses?

9.  How is skills training useful in helping people with specific interpersonal deficits?

10. In what ways are Albert Ellis's Rational-Emotive Therapy and Aaron Beck's Cognitive Therapy similar?

11. What is Albert Ellis's *ABC theory* of psychopathology?

12. What are the key assumptions of Gestalt therapy?

13. What are the key assumptions of Rogerian therapy?

14. In  what ways does group therapy differ from individual therapy? What are some advantages of group therapy approaches?

15. What is the focus of the *structural* and the *strategic* approaches to family therapy?

16. What are the assumptions underlying Murray Bowen's *intergenerational approach* to family therapy?

17. Compare how family-systems therapists, psychodynamic therapists, behavior therapists and cognitive-behavior therapists approach marital therapy.

18.   What psychotropic medication is effective with each of the following disorders? How does each medication work, and what are the drawbacks to its use?

Psychosis

Depression

Mania

Anxiety

19.   For what disorders is electroconvulsive therapy (ECT) effective? What are the pros and cons to the use of ECT?

20.   How are lobotomies accomplished? What are the consequences of this procedure?

21.   What has research shown concerning the relative effectiveness of psychodynamic, humanistic, and cognitive-behavioral therapies?

22.   What common factors underlie all therapies and may contribute to similar outcomes despite their different approaches?

23.   How do efficacy studies and efficiency studies differ? Why are both needed to evaluate psychotherapy?

24.    Why do some psychotherapists attempt to integrate therapies?

25.   What are the reasons for and consequences of deinstitutionalization of psychiatric patients?

## PART TWO:    REVIEW AND LEARN
## KEY TERMS, FILL-IN EXERCISES, APPLICATION AND USING WHAT YOU HAVE LEARNED

Before doing the exercises below, review the information you learned in this chapter. Reread the work you did in part one of this study guide chapter, plus the interim summaries and end-of-chapter summary in your textbook. Review any problem areas. Once you feel comfortable with the material, do the following exercises without referring to your notes or textbook. If you have difficulty with a term or question, mark it and come back to it. When you have finished an exercise, go back to your notes and the textbook to find the answers to the questions that gave you difficulty. Finally, check your answers (key terms against the textbook and the rest against the answer key).

## KEY TERMS

Insight _____

_____

Therapeutic alliance _____

_____

Free association _____

_____

Interpretation _____

_____

Resistance _____

_____

Transference _____

_____

Countertransference _____

_____

Psychoanalysis _____

_____

Psychodynamic psychotherapy _____

_____

Behavioral analysis _____

_____

Behavior therapy _____

_____

Systematic desensitization _____

_____

Exposure techniques _____

_____

Flooding _____

_____

Graded exposure _____

_____

Token economy _____

_____

Participatory modeling _____

_____

Skills training _____

_____

Social skills training _____

_____

Cognitive therapy _____

_____

Automatic thoughts _____

_____

Rational-emotive therapy _____

_____

ABC theory of psychopathology _____

_____

Humanistic therapies _____

_____

Gestalt therapy _____

_____

Empty-chair technique _____

_____

Client-centered therapy _____

_____

Unconditional positive regard _____

_____

Group therapy _____

_____

Group process _____

_____

Self-help group _____

_____

Family therapy _____

_____

Genogram _____

_____

Marital (or couples) therapy _____

_____

Psychotropic medications _____

_____

Antipsychotic medication _____

_____

Tricyclic antidepressants _____

_____

Monoamine oxidase (MAO) inhibitors _____

_____

Selective serotonin reuptake inhibitors (SSRIs) _____

_____

Lithium _____

_____

Benzodiazepines    _____

_____

Electroconvulsive therapy (ECT) _____

_____

Psychosurgery    _____

_____

Primary prevention _____

_____

## FILL-IN EXERCISES

Fill in the word or words that best fit in the spaces below.

1.  Understanding one's own psychological processes is referred to as _____.

2.  In psychodynamic treatment, the relationship between the patient and therapist, or therapeutic _____, is crucial for therapeutic change.

3.  _____ refers to barriers to free association or treatment that the patient creates.

4.  _____ refers to the situation in which the therapist-patient interaction triggers responses in the therapist.

5.  A procedure in which the patient mentally approaches a phobic stimulus gradually while in a relaxed state that inhibits anxiety is referred to as _____ _____.

6.  Confronting the phobic stimulus all at once is the behavior therapy technique of _____. A modification of this procedure that involves presenting real stimuli that are increasingly intense is called _____ _____.

7.  _____ _____ training is a behavioral procedure that has been devised for people with specific interpersonal deficits such as shyness or lack of assertiveness.

8.  Aaron Beck refers to the things people spontaneously say to themselves and the assumptions they may have as _____ thoughts.

9.    According to Albert Ellis, patients can rid themselves of unhappiness if they learn to maximize their _____ thinking and minimize their _____ thinking.

10.    According to Beck, people with anxiety disorders tend to _____ the probability and severity of the feared event and _____ their coping resources.

11.    To Gestalt therapists, understanding _____ one feels a certain way is far less important than recognizing _____ one feels that way.

12.    The *empty chair technique* is one of the best known procedures used by _____ therapists.

13.    Carl Rogers was among the first to refer to people who seek treatment as _____ rather than _____.

14.    Rogers stressed the curative value of _____, by which he meant becoming emotionally in tune with and understanding the patient's experience, without judging it.

15.    One of the oldest and best known _____-_____ groups is Alcoholics Anonymous.

16.    The focus of family therapy is on _____ rather than simply on content.

17.    The most serious side effect of antipsychotic medications is _____ _____.

18.    Antidepressant medications increase the amount of _____, _____ or both available in the synapses.

19.    Benzodiazepenes _____ the action of the neurotransmitter GABA.

20.    Some therapists choose psychotherapeutic techniques selectively to suit the individual, a practice referred to as _____ therapy, one strategy of psychotherapy integration.

## USING WHAT YOU HAVE LEARNED

Identify the type of therapy and/or approach associated with each of the following procedures.

1.    A therapist places an empty chair in front of the patient and has him imagine his ex-girlfriend is in the chair. The patient tells her how he felt when she broke up with him.

2.   A therapist works with a client to help him grow and mature, to help him experience himself as he really is. The therapist helps him identify feelings and offers him a supportive environment, expressing an attitude of fundamental acceptance without any strings attached.

3.   A therapist trains a patient in deep relaxation. She then presents the patient with a hierarchically ordered sequence of stimuli that frighten him.

4.   A therapist trains a patient to examine her irrational beliefs and the role they play in causing a negative emotional response. He demonstrates to the patient the illogic in her beliefs and then teaches her alternative ways of thinking.

5.   A therapist works with the patient to develop a map of her family over four generations, looking for similarities between her current problems and problems in the family's past.

6.   A patient visits his therapist 3 times a week. He lies on a couch, while she sits behind him. Often she instructs him to say whatever comes to mind -- thoughts, feelings, images, fantasies, memories, or wishes -- and to try to censor nothing.

## APPLICATION

**Situation**

A friend of yours has been having a bad time with anxiety. She's been experiencing severe episodes of panic, accompanied by hyperventilation, a racing heart beat, and feelings of dizziness. When the attacks occur, she's petrified, feeling certain that she's having a stroke. She feels sure that she's going to have a panic attack while driving the car and that she'll pass out, lose control of the car and kill herself and someone else. She feels safe only if she stays at home or close enough to home that she can quickly return there if an attack occurs. She's always checking her pulse, looking for "signs" that a panic attack is about to happen. She decides to ask her doctor to refer her for help.

**Questions to Answer**

1.   Based on what you've read in this chapter, what do you believe would be the most appropriate psychotherapeutic approach for her? Why?

2.   How would a therapist using this approach conceptualize her problems?

3.   What procedures would the therapist using this approach employ?

4.   Regardless of what approach her therapist follows, what important characteristics should he or she display?

5. Suppose pharmacotherapy were recommended for her. What type of medication would likely be effective?

6. What would be some of the drawbacks associated with pharmacotherapy alone?

# PART THREE:    TEST AND KNOW
# SAMPLE TEST QUESTIONS

Test how well you have learned this chapter's material by answering the sample test questions. You may wish to mark your answers on a separate sheet of paper so you can reuse this test for exam review. Once you have completed the exam, check your answers and then go back to your notes and the textbook to review questions you found difficult.

1. To bring about therapeutic change, psychodynamic psychotherapies rely on three techniques

   a. empathy, interpretation, and analysis of transference
   b. free association, interpretation, and collaborative empiricism
   c. interpretation, skills training, and unconditional positive regard
   d. free association, interpretation, and analysis of transference

2. Transference refers to

   a. the displacement of thoughts, feelings, fears, wishes, and conflicts from past relationships onto new relationships, especially with the therapist
   b. the replacement of a conditioned fear response with relaxation in the process of systematic desensitization
   c. how selective serotonin reuptake inhibitors (SSRIs) work at the synapse
   d. the process by which people with anxiety disorders overestimate the probability and severity of a feared event and underestimate their coping resources

3. The majority of clinical psychology faculty members at U.S. universities today are _____ in their orientation.

   a. psychodynamic
   b. client-centered
   c. cognitive-behavioral
   d. Gestalt

4.    The effectiveness of cognitive-behavioral therapies lies in their

    a.    ability to target specific psychological processes
    b.    use of empathy and unconditional positive regard
    c.    focus on the individual in the context of his or her family system
    d.    focus on helping the individual to express repressed feelings

5.    According to the cognitive-behavioral approach, phobic responses, like all avoidance responses, are

    a.    difficult to treat
    b.    particularly resistant to extinction
    c.    treatable using a token economy procedure
    d.    particularly treatable using a countertransference procedure

6.    A procedure in which the therapist demonstrates a behavior and then encourages the patient to engage in the same behavior is

    a.    social skills training        b.    graded exposure
    c.    participatory modeling      d.    counter-conditioning

7.    The "C" in Ellis's ABC theory of psychopathology refers to

    a.    belief systems
    b.    emotional consequences
    c.    activating conditions
    d.    unconscious conflicts

8.    Beck, like Ellis, views cognitive therapy as a process of _____ , in which patient and therapist work together testing hypotheses.

    a.    collaborative empiricism
    b.    counter-conditioning
    c.    experiencing one's true self
    d.    growing and maturing

9.    The goal of humanistic therapies is to

    a.    help people understand the internal workings of their mind and thus gain the capacity to make conscious, rational, adult choices
    b.    change maladaptive behavior patterns
    c.    help people to a realization of the role their thoughts play in emotional or mental unhappiness, ineffectuality, and disturbance
    d.    help people get in touch with their feelings, with their "true selves," and with a sense of meaning in life

10.    One of the most widely practiced humanistic therapies is

    a.    the intergenerational approach
    b.    rational-emotive therapy
    c.    family-systems therapy
    d.    client-centered therapy

11.    In Rogerian therapy, the therapist creates a supportive atmosphere by demonstrating _____ .

    a.    love and respect for the client
    b.    a therapeutic alliance with the client
    c.    unconditional positive regard for the client
    d.    collaborative empiricism to the client

12.    Self-help groups differ from other forms of group therapy in that they

    a.    are generally not guided by a professional
    b.    focus on a common issue or disorder
    c.    are insight oriented rather than behaviorally oriented
    d.    reduce the problem of transference as there is no leader

13.    The intergenerational approach of Murray Bowen employs _____ as an assessment technique.

    a.    interpretation
    b.    a genogram
    c.    free association
    d.    analysis of transference

14.    Techniques such as building communications skills, assertiveness training, and "good faith" contracts are used in marital therapy by

    a.    family-systems therapists
    b.    client-centered therapists
    c.    cognitive-behavioral therapists
    d.    psychodynamic therapists

15.    Antipsychotic medications are also sometimes called

    a.    benzodiazepines
    b.    selective serotonin reuptake inhibitors (SSRIs)
    c.    monoamine oxidase (MAO) inhibitors
    d.    major tranquilizers

16.    Antipsychotic medications inhibit the action of

   a.    monoamine oxidase
   b.    dopamine
   c.    serotonin
   d.    norepinephrine

17.    Tricyclic antidepressants

   a.    block the reuptake of serotonin and norepinephrine
   b.    keep the chemical monoamine oxidase from breaking down
         neurotransmitter substances in the presynaptic neuron
   c.    target serotonin rather than norepinephrine
   d.    are the treatment of choice for bipolar depression

18.    Fluoxetine (Prozac) is the best known

   a.    benzodiazepine
   b.    antipsychotic
   c.    selective serotonin reuptake inhibitor
   d.    monoamine oxidase inhibitor

19.    The main side effect of electroconvulsive therapy (ECT) is

   a.    memory loss
   b.    tardive dyskinesia
   c.    dry mouth, restlessness, agitation
   d.    weight gain, nausea, light-headedness

20.    ECT can sometimes be useful in treating _____, as well as depression.

   a.    anorexia
   b.    schizophrenia
   c.    mania
   d.    antisocial personality disorder

## ANSWERS

### FILL-IN EXERCISES

1. insight  2. alliance  3. resistance  4. countertransference  5. systematic desensitization
6. flooding; graded exposure  7. social skills  8. automatic  9. rational; irrational
10. overestimate; underestimate  11. why; that  12. Gestalt  13. clients; patients
14. empathy  15. self-help  16. process  17. tardive dyskinesia  18. norepinephrine,
serotonin  19. increase  20. eclectic

### APPLICATION

1. Cognitive-behavior therapy. Its effectiveness for anxiety is well established.
2. Panic attacks are the result of associating autonomic reactions with an impending
panic attack, leading to panic whenever these reactions occur. Feelings of helplessness
in the face of an impending attack, and catastrophic thoughts about consequences
compound the problem. Staying at home is the result of avoidance learning.
3. Paced breathing exercises; repeated exposure to experience of racing heart; rational
analysis of the accuracy of catastrophic beliefs.
4. Empathy; warm therapist-client relationship; instilling a sense of hope and efficacy.
5. Benzodiazepenes or antidepressants.
6. Possible physiological or psychological dependency.

### USING WHAT YOU HAVE LEARNED

1. Gestalt therapy (humanistic approaches) 2. client-centered therapy (humanistic
approaches)  3. systematic desensitization (behavior therapy)  4. rational-emotive
therapy (cognitive therapy)  5. intergenerational approach (family therapy)
6. psychoanalysis (psychodynamic approaches)

### SAMPLE TEST QUESTIONS

| 1.  | d | 11. | c |
|-----|---|-----|---|
| 2.  | a | 12. | a |
| 3.  | c | 13. | b |
| 4.  | a | 14. | c |
| 5.  | b | 15. | d |
| 6.  | c | 16. | b |
| 7.  | b | 17. | a |
| 8.  | a | 18. | c |
| 9.  | d | 19. | a |
| 10. | d | 20. | c |

# Chapter 17
# ATTITUDES AND SOCIAL COGNITION

## PART ONE: PRE-READ AND WORK
## OUTLINE AND LEARNING OBJECTIVES

Pre-read this chapter's table of contents and end-of-chapter summary. Then, use the outline segment-by-segment to help you work through the chapter. Jot down your own questions, comments, and notes in the space provided. Make a note of difficult areas that you will need to review (include page numbers). Then, answer the questions in the learning objectives section that follows. Check off those you are confident that you can answer well. Re-read the material in the text for the questions about which you are less confident. Record the important points from your reading in the space below each question.

## OUTLINE

I. ATTITUDES

A. The Nature of Attitudes

B. Attitudes and Behavior

C. Persuasion

D. Cognitive Dissonance

II. SOCIAL COGNITION

A. Social versus Nonsocial Cognition

D. Self-Consistency

E. **A Global Vista:** Culture and Self

## VI.  SOME CONCLUDING THOUGHTS

## LEARNING OBJECTIVES

Upon completion of Chapter 17, you should be able to answer the following questions.

1.    Differentiate between attitude strength and attitude accessibility.

2.    Explain what is meant by the cognitive and evaluative components of attitudes. How are these two concepts related in the notion of attitudinal coherence?

3.    What is attitudinal ambivalence?

4.    Why aren't attitudes strongly predictive of behavior?

5.    Under what circumstances are the central and the peripheral routes to persuasion more persuasive, according to the elaboration likelihood model?

6. Discuss each of the following components of persuasion distinguished by psychologists: source, message, channel, receiver.

7. What is the phenomenon of cognitive dissonance?

8. How does perception of choice, as well as size of rewards and punishments, influence the extent to which dissonance arises?

9. How do self-perception theory and self-presentation account for the phenomenon of cognitive dissonance?

10. Can it be said that cognitive dissonance is a culturally universal phenomenon?

11. In what four major ways does social cognition differ from nonsocial cognition?

12. How does attractiveness influence first impressions?

13. What is the role of schemas in social information processing?

14. How do stereotypes lead to prejudice?

15. How do the notions of scapegoating and the authoritarian personality explain prejudice?

16.   What is implicit racism, and how does this differ from a person's explicit attitudes?

17.   How can prejudice result from ingroup-outgroup distinctions?

18.   Why is contact alone insufficient to reduce intergroup hostility?

19.   What are three types of information people use in making internal or external attributions for behavior?

20.   How do discounting and augmentation influence attributions?

21.   What is correspondence bias and why is this particularly a phenomenon of contemporary Western culture?

22.   How can self-serving biases result in inaccurate social-information processing?

23.   What factors can cause biases in processing social information?

24.   What is the difference between the self as subject and self as object?

25.   Discuss the psychodynamic notion of self-representation.

26.   What are the emotional and physical consequences of discrepancies between (a) actual self and ideal self and (b) actual self and ought self?

27.    What is self-esteem? How do men and women differ in the way they derive self-esteem?

28.    How can the concept of "self" be considered culturally relative?

## PART TWO:    REVIEW AND LEARN
## KEY TERMS, FILL-IN EXERCISES, APPLICATION AND USING WHAT YOU HAVE LEARNED

Before doing the exercises below, review the information you learned in this chapter. Reread the work you did in part one of this study guide chapter, plus the interim summaries and end-of-chapter summary in your textbook.  Review any problem areas. Once you feel comfortable with the material, do the following exercises without referring to your notes or textbook.  If you have difficulty with a term or question, mark it and come back to it.  When you have finished an exercise, go back to your notes and the textbook to find the answers to the questions that gave you difficulty.  Finally, check your answers (key terms against the textbook and the rest against the answer key).

## KEY TERMS

Upon completion of Chapter 17, you should be able to define the following terms.

Attitude    _____

_____

Attitude strength    _____

_____

Attitude accessibility    _____

_____

Implicit attitude    _____

_____

Attitudinal ambivalence _____

_____

Attitudinal coherence _____

_____

Central route_____

_____

Peripheral route _____

_____

Elaboration likelihood model _____

_____

Persuasion _____

_____

Attitude inoculation _____

_____

Foot-in-the-door technique_____

_____

Cognitive dissonance _____

_____

Self-perception theory _____

_____

Self-presentation _____

_____

Social cognition   _____

_____

Halo effect   _____

_____

Person schemas   _____

_____

Situation schemas   _____

_____

Role schemas_____

_____

Relationship schemas   _____

_____

Stereotypes   _____

_____

Prejudice   _____

_____

Discrimination   _____

_____

Authoritarian personality   _____

_____

Implicit racism   _____

_____

Ingroup _____

_____

Outgroup _____

_____

External attribution _____

_____

Internal attribution _____

_____

Consensus _____

_____

Consistency _____

_____

Distinctiveness _____

_____

Discounting _____

_____

Augmentation _____

_____

Self-attribution _____

_____

Correspondence bias _____

_____

Self-serving bias   _____

_____

Self-concept  _____

_____

Self as subject   _____

_____

Self as object  _____

_____

Self-representations  _____

_____

Self-schema  _____

_____

Actual self  _____

_____

Ideal self  _____

_____

Ought self  _____

_____

Self-esteem  _____

_____

Self-consistency   _____

_____

## FILL-IN EXERCISES

Fill in the word or words that best fit in the spaces below.

1.  The statement "alcohol leads to major social problems" is an example of the _____ component of an attitude.

2.  Attitudinal _____ refers to the extent to which a given attitude object is associated with conflicting evaluative responses.

3.  Deliberate attempts to induce attitude change are referred to as _____.

4.  According to the elaboration likelihood model, the _____ route to persuasion is more effective when the person is both motivated and able to think about the arguments.

5.  Building up an individual's resistance to persuasion, by presenting weak arguments that are easily countered is referred to as _____ _____.

6.  _____ _____ occurs when a person experiences a discrepancy between an attitude and a behavior, or between an attitude and a new piece of information.

7.  _____-_____ theory holds that individuals infer their attitudes, emotions, and other internal states by observing their own behavior.

8.  _____ schemas represent information about what is expected of people in particular social positions.

9.  During times of economic recession, people search for _____ against which to target their displaced anger.

10. Prejudice requires a distinction between _____ and _____, that is, those who belong to the group and those who do not.

11. People tend to perceive members of _____ as much more homogeneous than they really are and to emphasize the individuality of _____ members.

12. The process of inferring the causes of one's own and others' mental states and behavior is referred to as _____.

13. The extent to which a person always responds in the same way to the same stimulus, referred to as _____, is one of several types of information that are important in attribution judgments.

14.    Increasing an internal attribution for behavior, despite situational pressures, is referred to as _____.

15.    Self as _____ refers to the person's experience of self as a thinker, feeler, and actor, whereas self as _____ is the person's view of himself or herself.

16.    Hopes, aspirations, and wishes that define the way a person would like to be, make up the _____ _____.

## APPLICATION

### Situation

Ms. Beagley is having some problems in her grade-7 class. Two cliques of girls have formed. These cliques have become increasingly hostile toward one another, with taunting, name calling, and verbal aggression on the rise. In her attempt to solve the problem, Ms. Beagley has rearranged the seating in her classroom, so that girls from each clique must be seatmates. So far, this hasn't worked. Instead, hostilities seem to have increased. When one girl accidentally spilled her seatmate's coke at lunch, she was immediately accused of doing it on purpose. "You and all your friends are the same. You're jerks!" she was told by her seatmate. When the same girl offered her science book to her seatmate who had forgotten hers, her seatmate's response was, "What choice did she have, teacher would've made her loan it to me anyway!" Ms. Beagley cannot figure out what is happening in her class. She calls upon you to help her understand why these girls are so antagonistic to one another and to brainstorm with her for ways to solve this problem.

### Questions to Answer

1.    From what you've read in Chapter 17, what do you think is going on in Ms. Beagley's class?

2.    What process do you think is at the root of the hostility and discrimination between these two groups of girls?

3.    What kind of errors or overgeneralizations can you see in how the girls in one clique view those in the other? How would you expect them to interpret positive and negative actions performed by members of their clique? How would they interpret the same behaviors performed by members of the other clique?

4.    Why hasn't Ms. Beagley's strategy of rearranging the seating plan been successful in resolving the hostilities? What would be a better way to reduce hostilities between the groups of girls?

# USING WHAT YOU HAVE LEARNED

Provide the correct label for the phenomena described in each of the following:

1.  Joanne is an extremely attractive woman. She is a tall, slim, well-dressed business woman. When they first meet her, most people automatically assume that she must be competent and confident.

2.  As they enter the room for their final exam, all the students know exactly what's expected of them. They leave their bags and books outside. They then find a seat and get out their pens, pencils, and erasers. They sit in their place quietly, without talking with any other students, and wait for the exam to begin.

3.  After hearing a vignette about a criminal attorney, most subjects recalled that he was shrewd and calculating, but few remembered the color of his briefcase.

4.  Hearing about the success of a gifted musician, whose father was also a very successful musician, one individual argued: "Oh well, she didn't have to work at it very hard. She's riding on her father's coat tails."

5.  Steve had to choose between psychology and dentistry. It was tough. He thought about it for a long time and then chose psychology. Afterward, he was told that dentists make a lot more money, and he began to ruminate about his choice. Then, he came across an article on the high incidence of stress-related illness in dentists. To ease his mind about his choice of psychology, he began reading all he could find about the stress dentists are under.

# PART THREE:   TEST AND KNOW
# SAMPLE TEST QUESTIONS

Test how well you have learned this chapter's material by answering the sample test questions.  You may wish to mark your answers on a separate sheet of paper so you can reuse this test for exam review.  Once you have completed the exam, check your answers and then go back to your notes and the textbook to review questions you found difficult.

1.  Social psychologists distinguish the following three components of an attitude

    a.   cognitive, evaluative, behavioral
    b.   conscious, unconscious, preconscious
    c.   cognitive, social, physical
    d.   self-concept, self-esteem, self-representation

2.    The best form of persuasion when an attitude is not strongly held and is based on minimal knowledge is to

   a.    induce the person to think carefully and weigh the arguments
   b.    encourage emotional responses that bypass the belief components of the attitude
   c.    overwhelm the person with so much information that he no longer even knows what the issue is
   d.    offer tangible incentives to the person to change her opinion

3.    Which of the following characteristics of a speaker play an important role in how successful her attempt at persuasion will be?

   a.    credibility                      b.    attractiveness
   c.    power                            d.    all of the above

4.    The "foot-in-the-door" technique is based on the principle that

   a.    if the person delivering a message shows obvious pain (as though her foot were caught in the door), the listener will have sympathy with her and will comply with her request
   b.    if the person delivering a message can get the listener's clear attention, the listener is more likely to comply
   c.    once people comply with a small request they are more likely to comply with one that is bigger
   d.    if someone has complied with a big request, he will almost automatically comply with a smaller one

5.    After Bill bought his new, name-brand computer, he came across an advertisement for a clone that had all the features of his new computer and cost half the price. Bill began to collect all the information he could find on the value of buying a name-brand computer. Bill's behavior was motivated by

   a.    social cognition
   b.    cognitive dissonance
   c.    an intuitive scientist approach
   d.    a halo effect

6.    Jacob is an accountant with a busy practice. He is tall and athletic. Just seeing him pass by on the street, people "know" he's a good accountant. This inference people make about Jacob's abilities is known as a

   a.    role schema                     b.    script
   c.    halo effect                     d.    relationship schema

7.  When Julie heard that her doctor was a champion motocross rider, she just couldn't believe it. Motocross riding just does not fit in her _____ for doctors.

    a.  script
    b.  halo
    c.  person schema
    d.  self-representation

8.  Which of the following is *not* true about social schemas?

    a.  They facilitate recall of schema-relevant social information.
    b.  They interfere with recall of information that is highly discrepant with the schema.
    c.  They organize encoding of social information.
    d.  They direct and guide social information processing.

9.  Schemas about the personal attributes of a group of people that are often overgeneralized, inaccurate, and resistant to new information are referred to as

    a.  outgroups
    b.  situation schemas
    c.  relationship schemas
    d.  stereotypes

10. The _____ personality refers to a particular personality style that is prone to hate people who are different or downtrodden.

    a.  antisocial
    b.  authoritative
    c.  borderline
    d.  authoritarian

11. Jane Elliot's classroom study in which she informed children that brown-eyed children are superior and blue-eyed children are inferior clearly demonstrated how

    a.  a distinction between ingroups and outgroups leads to prejudice
    b.  social schemas can be altered easily by simply presenting information that conflicts with the content of the schema
    c.  cognitive dissonance plays a major role in even the attitudes of school children
    d.  children are resistant to information that they know is wrong, even when it's presented by an adult authority figure

12.    Islam and Hewstone's (1993) study of how Hindu and Muslim students in Bangladesh explained the causes of helpful or unhelpful behavior presented in vignettes revealed which of the following?

   a.    Positive acts by ingroup members were attributed to environmental circumstances.
   b.    Positive acts by outgroup members were seen to reflect enduring personality attributes.
   c.    Negative acts by outgroup members were attributed to environmental circumstance.
   d.    Positive acts by ingroup members were seen to reflect enduring personality attributes.

13.    The study of the conflict between the Rattlers and Eagles groups at a Boy Scout summer camp showed that

   a.    extended contact between the two groups (i.e., bringing the two groups together for pleasant activities) was what was required to reduce conflict
   b.    there was nothing that could reduce conflict between the two groups
   c.    conflict between the two groups could only be reduced by terminating the camp
   d.    cooperation and contact between the two groups were required to reduce conflict

14.    In making attributions to the person or to the situation, people rely on which of the following types of information?

   a.    stereotypes, ingroups, outgroups
   b.    consensus, consistency, distinctiveness
   c.    cause, effect, correlation
   d.    discounting, augmenting, attributing

15.    "I know what Jerry said to you was mean" said Phil, "but, let's give him a break. He just found out he failed all his midterms." Phil's attribution for Jerry's behavior shows evidence of

   a.    consensus
   b.    augmentation
   c.    discounting
   d.    consistency

16.    Correspondence bias refers to

   a.    looking for information that fits with the way a person already views him/herself
   b.    the effects of first impressions on our judgments of people
   c.    the belief people hold that positive qualities tend to cluster together
   d.    the tendency to attribute behaviors to people's personalities and to ignore possible situational causes

17.    A majority of people rate themselves above average on most dimensions. This is, of course, statistically impossible, and is a good example of:

   a.    self-serving bias            b.    correspondence bias
   c.    augmentation               d.    self-consistency

18.    Emotions, such as fear, guilt, uneasiness, and self-contempt, which characterize anxious individuals, may the result of a discrepancy between

   a.    ideal self and ought self
   b.    actual self and ideal self
   c.    actual self and ought self
   d.    self as subject and self as object

19.    How do men and women differ in the way they derive self-esteem?

   a.    Men emphasize their capacity to connect with other people, whereas women emphasize their distinctiveness in comparison to others.
   b.    Women emphasize their capacity to connect with other people, whereas men emphasize their distinctiveness in comparison to others.
   c.    Men emphasize the self as object, whereas women emphasize the self as subject.
   d.    Women respond to threats to their self-esteem by comparing themselves to others who are worse on some dimension than themselves, whereas men exaggerate their positive social traits.

20.    Self-consistency refers to

   a.    people's tendency to perceive themselves in a manner consistent with the view of those around them
   b.    the ability to achieve a balance between the real, ideal, and ought selves
   c.    people's tendency to behave in a consistent manner across a variety of situations
   d.    people's tendency to interpret information to fit the way they see themselves and to prefer people who verify their view of themselves

# ANSWERS

## FILL-IN EXERCISES

1. cognitive (belief)  2. ambivalence  3. persuasion  4. central  5. attitude inoculation
6. cognitive dissonance  7. self-perception  8. role  9. scapegoats 10. ingroups,
outgroups  11. outgroups; ingroup  12. attribution  13. consistency 14. augmentation
15. subject; object  16. ideal self

## APPLICATION

1. Intergroup antagonism and prejudice
2. Ingroup-outgroup distinction
3. They perceive members of the outgroup as much more homogeneous than they
really are. They make the following attribution errors in explaining the behavior of
outgroup members: When considering the behavior of those not in their clique (i.e.,
outgroup members) the girls attribute positive behavior (one girl offering to share her
book) to environmental circumstances and negative behavior (spilling the coke) to
internal personality attributes. Most likely they would attribute positive and negative
behaviors performed by *ingroup* members to internal and external causes, respectively.
4. As was the case in the study with the Rattlers and Eagles at a boy scout camp, contact
alone is not enough to resolve conflict. The contact must also involve cooperation. Ms.
Beagley should create a situation that involves superordinate goals that require the two
groups to cooperate for the benefit of all.

## USING WHAT YOU HAVE LEARNED

1. halo effect  2. situation schema   3. social schema (or person schema)  4. discounting
5. cognitive dissonance

## SAMPLE TEST QUESTIONS

| 1.  | a | 11. | a |
|-----|---|-----|---|
| 2.  | b | 12. | d |
| 3.  | d | 13. | d |
| 4.  | c | 14. | b |
| 5.  | b | 15. | c |
| 6.  | c | 16. | d |
| 7.  | c | 17. | a |
| 8.  | b | 18. | c |
| 9.  | d | 19. | b |
| 10. | d | 20. | d |

# Chapter 18
# INTERPERSONAL PROCESSES

## PART ONE:   PRE-READ AND WORK
## OUTLINE AND LEARNING OBJECTIVES

Pre-read this chapter's table of contents and end-of-chapter summary.  Then, use the outline segment-by-segment to help you work through the chapter. Jot down your own questions, comments, and notes in the space provided. Make a note of key terms and of difficult areas that you will need to review (include page numbers). Then, answer the questions in the learning objectives section that follows. Check off those you are confident that you can answer well. Re-read the material in the text for the questions about which you are less confident. Record the important points from your reading in the space below each question.

## OUTLINE

I.   RELATIONSHIPS

    A. Factors Leading to Interpersonal Attraction

    B. Love

    C. **A Global Vista:** Love in Cross-Cultural Perspective

II.   ALTRUISM

    A. Theories of Altruism

B. Bystander Intervention

## III.  AGGRESSION

A. Violence and Culture

B. Violence and Gender

C. **One Step Further:** Why Men Rape

D. The Roots of Violence

E. **From  Mind to Brain:** The Biological Basis of Aggression

## IV.  SOCIAL INFLUENCE

A. Obedience

B. Conformity

C. Group Processes

## V.  SOME CONCLUDING THOUGHTS

## LEARNING OBJECTIVES

Upon completion of Chapter 18, you should be able to answer the following questions.

1. How does each of the following factors influence interpersonal attraction: proximity, interpersonal rewards, similarity, physical attractiveness?

2. What are the differences between passionate love and companionate love?

3. What three categories make up Robert Sternberg's triangular theory of love, and how do these interact to produce eight basic types of love?

4. What are the differences in "sexual strategies" of males and females, as described by the evolutionary perspective?

5. How do attachment theorists view romantic love?

6. How do the concepts of love and marriage differ across cultures and history?

7. How does the notion of ethical hedonism explain altruism?

8.    What do evolutionary psychologists mean by reciprocal altruism?

9.    How does the presence of others influence bystander intervention?

10.    How does the prevalence and form of aggression vary by culture and gender?

11.    What motivates the behavior of rapists? Describe the characteristics and background of serial rapists.

12.    What are the similarities and differences between the psychodynamic and evolutionary views of aggression?

13.    What neural and hormonal systems have been found to underlie aggressive behavior?

14.    How do television violence and pornography affect aggression?

15.    How does frustration lead to aggression? What environmental factors have been found to increase both aggression and frustration?

16.    What factors influence obedience, according to Milgram's research?

17.    How did Solomon Asch demonstrate the power of conformity?

18.    How do reference groups influence the norms to which people respond?

19.    How can people's attitudes and behavior be influenced by the roles they assume?

20.    What are several different roles that commonly emerge in groups?

21.    How do the following three leadership styles differ: autocratic, democratic, and laissez-faire?

22.    Explain the influence charismatic leaders hold over people.

## PART TWO:    REVIEW AND LEARN
## KEY TERMS, FILL-IN EXERCISES, APPLICATION AND USING WHAT YOU HAVE LEARNED

Before doing the exercises below, review the information you learned in this chapter. Reread the work you did in part one of this study guide chapter, plus the interim summaries and end-of-chapter summary in your textbook. Review any problem areas. Once you feel comfortable with the material, do the following exercises without referring to your notes or textbook. If you have difficulty with a term or question, mark it and come back to it. When you have finished an exercise, go back to your notes and the textbook to find the answers to the questions that gave you difficulty. Finally, check your answers (key terms against the textbook and the rest against the answer key).

## KEY TERMS

Altruism  _____

_____

Interpersonal attraction  _____

_____

Social exchange theories  _____

_____

Passionate love  _____

_____

Companionate love  _____

_____

Sexual strategies  _____

_____

Ethical hedonism  _____

_____

Reciprocal altruism _____

_____

Bystander intervention     _____

_____

Diffusion of responsibility _____

_____

Aggression _____

_____

Instrumental aggression     _____

_____

Frustration-aggression hypothesis     _____

_____

Social influence     _____

_____

Social facilitation     _____

_____

Obedience     _____

_____

Conformity _____

_____

Group Norms     _____

_____

Reference groups _____

_____

Status _____

_____

Role _____

_____

Task leader _____

_____

Social-emotional leader _____

_____

Tension-release role_____

_____

Leader _____

_____

Autocratic leadership style_____

_____

Democratic leadership style _____

_____

Laissez-faire leadership style _____

_____

Charismatic leader _____

_____

## FILL-IN EXERCISES

Fill in the word or words that best fit in the spaces below.

1.   Helping another person with no apparent gain to oneself is referred to as
_____.

2.   Social exchange theories hold that the foundation of relationships is _____
reward.

3.   Whereas _____ love is marked by intense physiological arousal and absorption
in another person, _____ love involves deep affection, friendship, and
emotional intimacy.

4.   According to evolutionary psychologists, short-term and long-term mating
strategies are similar for _____ (males/females).

5.   Perceived similarity of the victim to the bystander _____ the likelihood of
intervention, because it maximizes _____.

6.   Calm, pragmatic aggression is referred to as _____ aggression.

7.   Electrical stimulation of the lateral _____ results in attack behavior in cats or
rhesus monkeys.

8.   Although viewing pornography does not _____ sexual violence, viewing
pornographic *aggression* does appear to _____ men to the brutality of sexual
violence.

9.   Recent thinking suggests that frustration leads to aggression, to the extent that a
frustrating event elicits unpleasant _____.

10.  Within countries as diverse as Spain, Italy, France, and the United States, the
southern regions typically have the highest rates of _____ crime.

11.  Social _____ refers to the performance-enhancing effects of the presence of
others.

12.  Milgram's research reveals that people will obey, without limitations of
conscience, if they believe an order comes from a legitimate _____.

13.  Solomon Asch's research demonstrated the powerful influence of _____.

14.    The _____ _____ is the group member who takes responsibility for seeing that the group completes its tasks.

15.    In Kurt Lewin's study where groups of boys made crafts after school, the style of leadership that led to neither satisfaction nor efficiency was a _____ style.

## APPLICATION

**Situation**

Jan is a 10th grader who has just moved to a new school, midway through the term. She immediately strikes up a friendship with Ruth, the girl whose locker is beside hers. Ruth doesn't appear to have many friends and seems to really enjoy Jan's company. During her first week at the new school, Jan had lunch with Ruth every day. As she gets to know the other girls, however, Jan discovers that nobody likes Ruth. Everyone agrees that it's not cool to be seen with Ruth, although nobody really knows why. As Jan feels more and more comfortable with her new classmates, she feels more and more pressure to reject Ruth. Sitting with some of her classmates one day, the conversation turns to Ruth. All the other girls agree that she's a "loser." Someone then asks Jan what she thinks about Ruth. She wants to stand up for Ruth, yet at the same time, she wants to be accepted by her new classmates. So she agrees that Ruth is a loser.[*]

**Questions to Answer**

1.    What is the phenomenon underlying Jan's dilemma?

2.    What factors lead to Jan's agreeing with the opinion of the group, despite her personal feelings to the contrary?

3.    Would it make any difference if another classmate had stood up for Ruth before they asked Jan what she thought?

4.    What is the term that would describe the unspoken rule among the girls in Jan's class that it's not cool to be seen with Ruth?

5.    Why would this group of girls be labeled a *positive* reference group for Jan in view of their behavior?

---

[*] This situation was derived from Hanna, J. & Younger, A. (1991, April). *Peer rejection and conformity.* Paper presented at the biennial meeting of the Society for Research in Child Development, Seattle, WA.

# USING WHAT YOU HAVE LEARNED

You have been asked to write a short article for the college newspaper on the topic of love and romance. The article is intended to dispel common myths and to present a psychological perspective on the topic. The editors want you to focus on the following points. Based on what you've read in Chapter 18, what would you say on each of these topics?

1.    What is it that attracts couples to each other?

2.    How important is physical attractiveness for love and romance?

3.    Are there different kinds of love?

4.    Are men and women looking for the same things in romance?

5.    How important is romance to marriage?

# PART THREE:    TEST AND KNOW
# SAMPLE TEST QUESTIONS

Test how well you have learned this chapter's material by answering the sample test questions. You may wish to mark your answers on a separate sheet of paper so you can reuse this test for exam review. Once you have completed the exam, check your answers and then go back to your notes and the textbook to review questions you found difficult.

1.    Proximity, similarity, attractiveness, and degree to which an interaction is rewarding are factors that influence

    a.    interpersonal attraction
    b.    reference groups
    c.    self-esteem
    d.    leadership

2.    Sternberg's triangular theory of love involves the following categories

    a.    passionate and companionate
    b.    intimacy, passion, and decision/commitment
    c.    physical and emotional
    d.    romantic love, friendship, and acquaintanceship

3.    Attachment theorists argue that

  a.    insecurely attached infants will never be able to develop adult romantic relationships
  b.    while secure attachment in infancy is predictive of secure romantic relationships in adulthood, nothing can be predicted from insecure attachment relationships
  c.    adult romantic relationships are *not* related to mother-infant attachment
  d.    people pattern their romantic relationships on the mental models they constructed of earlier attachment relationships

4.    The notion that all behavior, no matter how altruistic it appears to be, is designed to increase one's own pleasure or reduce one's own pain is referred to as

  a.    ethical hedonism
  b.    reciprocal altruism
  c.    diffusion of responsibility
  d.    instrumental altruism

5.    Darley and Latane developed a three-stage model of the decision-making process underlying bystander intervention. During stage 3, the presence of others

  a.    serves as an informational source (i.e., "is there a crisis here or isn't there?")
  b.    serves as a source of reassurance
  c.    serves to increase empathic distress in the bystander
  d.    leads to a diffusion of responsibility

6.    Which of the following is *not* among the characteristics common to serial rapists?

  a.    a history of prior sexual offenses
  b.    a history of unemployment
  c.    a history of antisocial behavior
  d.    a history of sexual abuse

7.    Most contemporary psychodynamic psychologists view aggression as

  a.    a basic instinct in humans
  b.    a class of behaviors that societies implant through social learning
  c.    an inborn behavioral potential usually activated by frustration and anger
  d.    behavior that is pleasurable only to sadists, delinquents, and antisocial personalities

8.    Across species, overt female aggression is largely elicited by

   a.    the mating attempts of a male when the female is unreceptive
   b.    competition between females for the same male
   c.    intrusion into their territory by another female
   d.    attacks on their young

9.    Electrical stimulation of the _____ can result in aggression and hostility in humans.

   a.    gonads
   b.    hippocampus
   c.    amygdala
   d.    cerebellum

10.    Which of the following is likely *not* a result of watching violent television programs?

   a.    increased arousal
   b.    increased inhibition
   c.    exposure to aggressive models
   d.    desensitization to violence

11.    Violent crimes such as rape, assault, murder, as well as prison unrest peak

   a.    during the spring because of the increase in testosterone levels in men
   b.    during the summer months when it is hot
   c.    during the fall when the imminent onset of winter leads to frustration
   d.    during the winter when daylight hours are shortest

12.    Dollard and Miller proposed that when people become _____, they become aggressive.

   a.    frustrated
   b.    obedient
   c.    charismatic
   d.    hedonistic

13.    In Milgram's research which of the following led to a decrease in obedience?

   a.    moving the victim to a separate room from the subject
   b.    moving the experimenter to the same room as the subject.
   c.    the presence of dissenters who refused to obey the experimenter
   d.    the presence of confederates who gave incorrect answers

14. If an adolescent shoplifts in order to be like her friends, her friends represent a

    a. positive influence
    b. negative reference group
    c. positive reference group
    d. social-emotional leader

15. In Asch's research where subjects indicated which lines were of matching length

    a. if even one of the confederates gave an incorrect answer, the majority of subjects conformed in their choices
    b. if three or more confederates gave incorrect answers, the majority of subjects conformed in their choices
    c. if three or more confederates gave incorrect answers, approximately half of the subjects conformed in their choices
    d. if at least one confederate gave a different answer than the others, participants followed their own judgments most of the time

16. The group member who tries to keep the group working cohesively and with minimum animosity is referred to as the

    a. task leader
    b. charismatic leader
    c. tension-release leader
    d. social-emotional leader

17. Zimbardo's research in which students played roles of prison inmates and guards showed that

    a. roles can actually influence social behavior
    b. because the roles were hypothetical, the students did not take them seriously
    c. roles have little influence on social behavior
    d. social behavior likely affects the roles people choose

18. In Kurt Lewin's study where groups of boys made crafts after school, the style of leadership that led to efficiency but also discontent was a _____ style.

    a. autocratic
    b. democratic
    c. laissez-faire
    d. permissive

19.    The personality dimensions characteristic of successful leaders are

   a.    extroversion and stubbornness
   b.    extroversion, risk-taking, and friendliness
   c.    persuasiveness, meekness, and cheerfulness
   d.    extroversion, agreeableness, conscientiousness

20.    A leader who inspires obedience by the force of his or her personality is referred to as

   a.    a social-emotional leader
   b.    an instrumental leader
   c.    a charismatic leader
   d.    a democratic leader

# ANSWERS

## FILL-IN EXERCISES

1. altruism  2. reciprocal  3. passionate; companionate  4. females  5. increases; empathy  6. instrumental  7. hypothalamus  8. cause; desensitize 9. affect  10. violent  11. facilitation  12. authority  13. conformity  14. task leader  15. laissez-faire

## APPLICATION

1. *Conformity.* As in Asch's studies on judgments of line length, this situation involves an individual who is confronted with opinions that differ from hers. Jan likes Ruth. But her classmates agree that it's not cool to like Ruth. So Jan changes her opinion to conform to the group.

2. What led to it was amount of opposition and need for social approval. Jan is a new student who wants to be accepted into her new peer group. Because her classmates unanimously agree that it's not cool to be Ruth's friend, Jan suppresses her opinion that Ruth is her friend, and conforms to the group opinion to gain their approval.

3. Yes. In Asch's studies, if even one confederate allied himself with the subject, the participants were more likely to stick with their original opinion. If one classmate had stood up for Ruth, it is likely that Jan would have stuck to her original opinion about Ruth.

4. A *norm.* All groups develop norms, or standards for behavior. This group of girls has an unspoken standard that it is not cool to be seen with Ruth.

5. The group is a *positive* reference group because Jan tries to emulate its members and meet their standards.

## SAMPLE TEST QUESTIONS

| | | | |
|---|---|---|---|
| 1. | a | 11. | b |
| 2. | b | 12. | a |
| 3. | d | 13. | c |
| 4. | a | 14. | c |
| 5. | d | 15. | d |
| 6. | b | 16. | d |
| 7. | c | 17. | a |
| 8. | d | 18. | a |
| 9. | c | 19. | d |
| 10. | b | 20. | c |

# NOTES

# NOTES

# NOTES

# NOTES

# NOTES

# NOTES

# NOTES

# NOTES

# NOTES